**New Directions for
Community Colleges**

Arthur M. Cohen
EDITOR-IN-CHIEF

Caroline Q. Durdella
Nathan R. Durdella
ASSOCIATE EDITORS

Supporting
Student Affairs
Professionals

C. Casey Ozaki
Anne M. Hornak
Christina J. Lunceford
EDITORS

Number 166 • Summer 2014
Jossey-Bass
San Francisco

SUPPORTING STUDENT AFFAIRS PROFESSIONALS
C. Casey Ozaki, Anne M. Hornak, Christina J. Lunceford (eds.)
New Directions for Community Colleges, no. 166

Arthur M. Cohen, Editor-in-Chief
Caroline Q. Durdella, Nathan R. Durdella, Associate Editors

NEW DIRECTIONS FOR COMMUNITY COLLEGES (ISSN 0194-3081, electronic ISSN 1536-0733) is part of The Jossey-Bass Higher and Adult Education Series and is published quarterly by Wiley Subscription Services, Inc., A Wiley Company, at Jossey-Bass, One Montgomery St., Ste. 1200, San Francisco, CA 94104. POSTMASTER: Send address changes to New Directions for Community Colleges, Jossey-Bass, One Montgomery St., Ste. 1200, San Francisco, CA 94104.

SUBSCRIPTIONS cost $89 for individuals in the U.S., Canada, and Mexico, and $113 in the rest of the world for print only; $89 in all regions for electronic only; $98 in the U.S., Canada, and Mexico for combined print and electronic; $122 for combined print and electronic in the rest of the world. Institutional print only subscriptions are $311 in the U.S., $351 in Canada and Mexico, and $385 in the rest of the world; electronic only subscriptions are $311 in all regions; combined print and electronic subscriptions are $357 in the U.S., $397 in Canada and Mexico, and $431 in the rest of the world.

EDITORIAL CORRESPONDENCE should be sent to the Editor-in-Chief, Arthur M. Cohen, at 1749 Mandeville Lane, Los Angeles, CA 90049. All manuscripts receive anonymous reviews by external referees.

New Directions for Community Colleges is indexed in CIJE: Current Index to Journals in Education (ERIC), Contents Pages in Education (T&F), Current Abstracts (EBSCO), Ed/Net (Simpson Communications), Education Index/Abstracts (H. W. Wilson), Educational Research Abstracts Online (T&F), ERIC Database (Education Resources Information Center), and Resources in Education (ERIC).

Microfilm copies of issues and articles are available in 16mm and 35mm, as well as microfiche in 105mm, through University Microfilms Inc., 300 North Zeeb Road, Ann Arbor, MI 48106-1346.

CONTENTS

Editors' Notes

Student affairs, as a profession, has come a long way in the development of its professional identity and foundations since its earliest origins. What was originally the organization and development for those who supported and worked with college students has evolved into an organized body of professionals with a foundational literature base and guiding standards (McClellan & Stringer, 2009). The field of student affairs has since been recognized as an integral partner in college students' experiences, learning, and overall success (McClellan & Stringer, 2009). The evolution of student affairs as a field and recognition of its role in student success underscores its importance in the effort to provide quality education to college students.

Higher education has more recently experienced increased pressure to demonstrate its student outcomes, learning, and success in an effort to monitor and ensure quality education (Arum & Roksa, 2011). This effort has been framed as the pursuit of excellence in higher education, emphasizing the importance of this goal across all institutional types and educational services, calling for the assessment of quality and outcomes (Astin & antonio, 2012). Critical to developing and supporting quality and effective student affairs practitioners are the knowledge and skills needed for professionals as they move through the career pipeline. Informing and shaping the fundamental education and experiences that professionals need for development are the field's professional guiding principles. Most notable are the standards and guidelines used to shape the profession and institutions, the professional preparation of individuals in the profession, and the ongoing support and development of professionals throughout their careers.

Two-year institutions have in recent years garnered attention as a primary gateway to postsecondary education for a diverse population of incoming and returning students (Cohen, Brawer, & Kisker, 2013). Reflecting the national conversation on assessment and excellence, community colleges are experiencing scrutiny of their student outcomes. Given the diverse needs across significant numbers of students in community colleges, student services professionals at these institutions are critical to this mission, yet are rarely a focus of discussion or research.

Across higher education, student services professionals and student affairs as a field of research and practice have focused on four-year institutions and traditional-aged college student experiences, yet nearly half of U.S. college students have or are currently attending two-year institutions. While much of the research and practice can be applied to student services

New Directions for Community Colleges, no. 166, Summer 2014 © 2014 Wiley Periodicals, Inc.
Published online in Wiley Online Library (wileyonlinelibrary.com) • DOI: 10.1002/cc.20095

at community colleges, they generally fail to acknowledge the broad range of responsibilities and diversity of students. Hirt's (2006) characterization of professional life at community colleges recognizes their broad missions and local focus resulting in "incredible workload for those employed at such institutions and leads [Hirt] to refer to student services professionals on these campuses as 'producers'" (p. 136). A recent mixed methods study of student affairs professionals at two-year institutions supported the perception that work in these institutions is unique to student affairs practice at most two-year institutions, requiring focused education, training, and skills (Lunceford, Ozaki, & Hornak, 2012). Given the unique work of community college student services professionals and the lack of focus and research on best practices for their work, the preparation, training, and professional development available to this sector of student affairs is lacking. A discussion of research and best practices specific to student services practitioners at two-year institutions is needed in order to support the quality and efficacy of their work.

Supporting Student Affairs Professionals offers a timely, much-needed practical discussion of the educational and professional practices and external influences (i.e., standards, competencies, and accreditation) whose purposes are to enhance and advance the quality and outcomes of student affairs work. The volume begins with an exploration and rationale for how the goal of excellence in community college student affairs influences the development and support of professionals along their career pipeline. Chapters 2–4 offer insight into the different levels of administrative and managerial roles (i.e., new professionals, mid-managers, and senior officers), exploring critical elements such as professional identity, development, and organizational behavior. In Chapter 5, the author turns the reader's attention to external influences designed to support and promote quality professionals. The following two chapters expand the discussion with a focused exploration of how professional competencies (Chapter 6) and accreditation (Chapter 7) shape and inform professional and institutional quality. Chapter 8 draws from the dialogue across chapters to provide recommendations and suggestions for practice. The volume concludes with a discussion of student affairs from an organizational perspective, focusing on the intersections and collaborations necessary to provide excellence for student learning.

C. Casey Ozaki
Anne M. Hornak
Christina J. Lunceford
Editors

References

Arum, R., & Roksa, J. (2011). *Academically adrift: Limited learning on college campuses.* Chicago, IL: University of Chicago Press.

Astin, A. W., & antonio, a. l. (2012). *Assessment for excellence: The philosophy and practice of assessment and evaluation in higher education* (2nd ed.). New York, NY: Roman & Littlefield.

Cohen, A. M., Brawer, F. B., & Kisker, C. B. (2013). *The American community college* (6th ed.). San Francisco, CA: Jossey-Bass.

Hirt, J. B. (2006). *Where you work matters: Student affairs administration at different types of institutions.* Lanham, MD: University Press of America.

Lunceford, C., Ozaki, C. C., & Hornak, A. M. (2012, November). *Exploring preparation and the use of standards for student affairs professionals in community colleges.* Paper presented at the annual conference of the Association for the Study of Higher Education, Las Vegas, NV.

McClellan, G. S., & Stringer, J. (2009). *The handbook of student affairs administration.* San Francisco, CA: Jossey-Bass.

C. CASEY OZAKI *is an assistant professor of teaching and learning at the University of North Dakota.*

ANNE M. HORNAK *is an associate professor of educational leadership at Central Michigan University.*

CHRISTINA J. LUNCEFORD *is an assistant professor of higher education and student affairs at Bowling Green State University.*

1

Student success, accountability, and educational outcomes have been strongly emphasized in U.S. community colleges in recent years. For those individuals serving in community college student affairs, intentional commitment to standards and competencies in professional practice is essential in order to achieve institutional expectations and to meet increasing external demands. Student affairs leaders must provide structure and support to staff members along the continuum of experience from emerging student affairs professionals to mid-level practitioners through senior-level executives in order to identify potential leaders and to develop succession plans for the community colleges of tomorrow. This chapter explores the framework of excellence in the support, preparation, and ongoing professional development of community college student affairs professionals.

Excellence in Community College Student Affairs

Ashley Knight

Community college leaders in this decade are focused on student success and educational outcomes like never before. For student affairs professionals, increased scrutiny from both inside and outside the institution has enhanced the interest in meeting measurable goals in both student success and professional practice. Focus on standards and competencies is one method of assessing effectiveness in student affairs work, but to achieve excellence entails going much further above the baseline of a particular standard or competency. Exploring the definition of excellence in general and in relation to student affairs work in community colleges may be in order.

To excel at something, one is considered exceptionally good, proficient, outstanding, and surpassing others who attempt the same activity. Achieving excellence in any field is more than meeting essential standards set by that profession; instead, it implies doing better than others or producing a higher quality outcome than those in the same field. Durant (1926/1961), in his summation of Aristotle's writings on excellence, wrote:

> Excellence is an art won by training and habituation: we do not act rightly be-
> cause we have virtue or excellence, but we rather have these because we have
> acted rightly; these virtues are formed in man by his doing the actions; we are
> what we repeatedly do. Excellence, then, is not an act but a habit. (p. 76)

Excellence, by this standard, is achieved by repeated right actions habitually utilized in a profession. Those who excel in an activity or field have
repeatedly acted in a way that results in an artful or virtuous outcome.

The word has been used in business and management circles, finding
traction in the early 1980s with Peters and Waterman's (1983) *In Search
of Excellence: Lessons from America's Best-Run Companies*. Since then, professionals in every field have attempted to quantify exemplary practices in
order to set the bar at the highest level for those seeking models of excellence in each vocation.

The term excellence in higher education has often focused on outcomes assessment and student success by accrediting bodies. While this
is one application of the term, the excellence perspective in this body of
work is focused on ways of being and doing that drive institutional practices that will measurably enhance student learning. The concept applies
to individuals and institutions of higher education that value effectiveness
and continuous improvement and that expect the highest quality outcomes
from educational programs and services.

Excellence is developed in community college student affairs professionals through consistent application of the kinds of actions that are
termed best practices or promising practices. Taking it one step further,
evidence-based practices are the gold standard, and these are found in institutions that habitually measure and assess the results of their actions.

A college that exudes best practices and intentionally uses collected
results to improve student learning and development (Palomba & Banta,
1999) is one that has adopted the excellence perspective. Astin and antonio
(2012) describe the higher education system as having "three basic goals:
education, research, and public or community service" (p. 4). They point
out that of these three goals, community colleges put more emphasis on
community service but that education remains the central focus of the system and that "the basic purpose of assessing students is to enhance their
educational development" (p. 4). Promoting excellence in the community
college means we are committed to delivering education that will improve
our students' educational development and their lives, and as a result will
improve our communities. Preparing and supporting community college
student affairs professionals to meet these expectations requires a commitment to the excellence perspective.

Graduate Student Preparation for Entry-Level Positions

Graduate student preparation for entry-level student affairs positions in
community colleges must begin with a focus on the competencies agreed

upon by the profession (ACPA/NASPA, 2010; Council for the Advancement of Standards in Higher Education, 2012). For graduates of those programs that emphasize counseling, student development theory, or higher education theory, attaining professional competencies through assistantships and internships is essential. A study of entry-level student affairs professionals who had completed a master's degree in the field found that preparation programs can better meet the expectations of student affairs leaders by ensuring new professionals have attained the skills of staff supervision, budgeting, strategic planning, and computer usage in addition to the preparation they receive in communication, ethics, multicultural awareness, problem solving, and programming (Waple, 2006). Attention to these skills more effectively prepares graduate students for their first jobs in student affairs.

Assessing Professionals for Excellence

Competencies and standards give us a sort of plumb line by which to consider our progress as student affairs professionals. They give us measurement tools to assess others and ourselves alongside our peers in the profession, and they remind us of the goals we must establish to improve our practice progressively over time. The Council for the Advancement of Standards in Higher Education standards and guidelines were written to guide professionals not only in program review and developing new programs but also to enhance staff development efforts on our campuses. As leaders and managers seek effective ways to evaluate and develop staff members, these guidelines can be the starting point in staff development. The excellence perspective demands that we not only meet but also exceed the standards and guidelines established by our profession.

Assessing our faculty and staff through the lens of the excellence perspective pushes our institutions to improve student learning and student success. Providing feedback to faculty and staff helps them to become more skilled student affairs practitioners, which effectively enhances the programs we offer to benefit students. This is another example of Astin's I–E–O (input–environment–outcome) model at work, as Astin and antonio (2012) write, "a basic function of assessment, then, is to provide feedback that will enhance the practitioners' understanding of the connections between their actions (the environment) and the talent development process (student outcomes)" (p. 141). Effective assessment elevates our work, both individually and collectively.

Developing Professionals for Excellence

Besides the professional development acquired by being employed and working day-to-day in the field, there are two primary methods of development for community college personnel: targeted professional development activities and mentoring efforts. Campus leaders can implement these

NEW DIRECTIONS FOR COMMUNITY COLLEGES • DOI: 10.1002/cc

formally and informally while using the results of these activities to identify future leaders and plan for succession over time.

Professional development can be formal and structured, as in attending workshops and conferences through professional organizations, but also through on-campus, in-service opportunities for growth. Leaders may schedule seminars and other training opportunities by taking advantage of competencies and strengths of other experts on campus, whether it is related to the dynamic legal landscape in higher education, leading edge technological advancement, or discussions on diversity and inclusion. An effort being made on numerous community college campuses is that of generating homegrown leadership schools to develop employees from various employment groups toward greater responsibility (Thompson, 2013). This kind of training and succession planning helps to identify emerging leaders and gives employees from entry-level and mid-level positions the opportunity to work alongside senior leadership in the pursuit of individual and institutional excellence.

Formal and informal mentoring enhances the development of student affairs practitioners. In Rodkin's (2011) study on leadership preparation for senior student affairs officers (SSAOs) at community colleges, he found that 82.6% of the 308 SSAOs surveyed indicated they had formed a mentoring relationship within the employment arena, but only 24.7% of those were considered a formal mentoring relationship (p. 132). The study indicates mentoring relationships enhanced leadership preparation for SSAOs in "organizational strategy, collaboration, community college advocacy, and professionalism" (p. 138). Mentoring relationships were found to be the "third most discussed" leadership development experience, behind the SSAOs student affairs work experience and specific leadership workshops through professional organizations or institution-based leadership programs (p. 143). Student affairs practitioners seeking excellence in preparation for more senior roles enhance their preparation through formal and informal mentoring relationships.

Recommendations for Developing Student Affairs Professionals for Excellence

Developing entry-level and mid-level student affairs staff can be one of the most rewarding elements of any leader's professional work. To accomplish effective staff development through the lens of the excellence perspective, a leader should embody the following ideals: exemplify excellence, communicate thoroughly, and provide opportunity.

Exemplify Excellence.   The foundational concept is that the leader must exemplify the behavior and professional characteristics he or she expects. Despite many years of experience and accomplishments, the senior leader must work harder than the rest of the team in order to model the expansive work ethic necessary for more junior members to prepare for a career that allows them to surpass others. The leader's behavior must match the expectations being made of others, from effort to outcomes to personal interactions. The leader must steep all departmental and divisional activities in current leadership and student development literature in order to maintain currency with evidence-based practices. One must take one's own professional development seriously including informal and lifelong learning strategies, which according to Cloud (2010) include "professional reading, personal reflection, travel, writing for publication, and active involvement in professional organizations" (p. 75). Simply, a leader must take the idiom "practice what you preach" to heart in order to develop excellence in his or her team.

Communicate Thoroughly. No matter where one is in the organizational chart, messages from the top must be communicated in a timely manner to every level. Anything less frustrates morale and limits the usefulness and impact of the message. Providing clear expectations of what it means to be successful with supervisors and senior leadership inspires a shared vision and reduces confusion and conflict for staff members. Every community college has a set of essential themes that bear repeating in every setting and with every employee group, whether those themes are related to the mission, vision, core values, or strategic directions of the college. If, for example, it is important that all employees participate in campus-wide initiatives in order to enhance shared governance efforts, and if employees will be evaluated according to their level of participation, this message should be repeated by individual supervisors as well as in internal campus communications, such as newsletters, employee portal pages, and staff meetings.

Another element of thorough communication is providing a high level of accessibility to information. College-wide information can be placed on the employee portal, or as is becoming more expected in this era of accountability, much information can be deposited on the college website. Important documents such as the results of a consultant's visit or a major task force's final report should be housed electronically in a visible location. Additionally, divisional and departmental employees expect accessibility to common documents, such as schedules, deadlines, agendas, and meeting minutes or notes, and these can be placed on a staff shared drive to promote excellent communication.

Thorough communication also entails responsiveness to others' phone calls and emails. While it is not uncommon for a community college administrator to receive 100 emails a day or more, once the vendor emails are eliminated it should still be feasible to respond within the commonly accepted timeframe of 24 hours or less. This essential commitment to excellence builds trust between individuals and departments, and promotes institutional effectiveness.

Finally, a community college student affairs professional who exemplifies excellence is one who takes time to build relationships with others and fosters a collegial work environment. Beyond the friendly greetings that are appreciated by everyone from the maintenance worker to the provost, sharing an interest in a staff member's video of her newly adopted kitten may be one of the few times a supervisor and staff member interact beyond the transactional nature of their work together and may go a long way in the employee's positive impressions of the leader. Excellence in preparing and supporting professionals to meet the needs of students requires a holistic approach and demands relational excellence in both large and small ways.

Provide Opportunity. The development of student affairs professionals requires a safe environment for practice, success, and failure in which they can take greater and greater steps toward proficiency and excellence. These opportunities to practice leadership and skills must be married with meaningful work experiences to develop projects they find inspirational. In order to be prepared for more senior-level positions, those with leadership potential must be given practical opportunities to direct personnel, budgets, and other resources.

The most elementary beginning for staff supervision comes with the direction of student work aides, and depending on the department may be recreation aides, office helpers, or even peer mentors or new student orientation leaders. After the professional develops basic supervision skills with undergraduate students, the department can reach out to graduate programs with internship opportunities that are supervised by the mid-level professional. The SSAO should remain a visible and accessible member of the supervision team, but can guide the mid-level professional toward excellence in directing and managing others. The excellence perspective has tremendous impact in the realm of human resources management, and it requires concentrated attention to legal, ethical, and interpersonal competencies over the span of one's career.

Directing budgetary and organizational resources provides growing professionals with the opportunity to learn, question, and test their proficiency for more responsible positions in the future. The SSAO can not only provide them with a portion of the budget to oversee and assist in goal setting but also allow for personal agency as they make fiscal decisions they believe will impact student success. A mid-level professional can be appointed lead on a particular software purchase and can interact with the various information technology staff, both internal and external to the college, which will improve the professional's knowledge and skills as well as broaden his or her understanding of the professional development necessary to be elevated to a more responsible position in the future.

Excellence in community college leadership is more than capably managing people, money, and things. It is, after all, taking responsibility for the college or a group within the college and moving it to greater accomplishments that will improve the educational outcomes for students. In the community college, much of this is done through shared governance, committee meetings and task forces, and departmental work groups. To develop student affairs professionals for this type of transcending leadership, the SSAO must provide opportunities for them to participate in college-wide committees as a representative of student affairs, to lead subgroups or task forces within the division, and to lead staff meetings in the SSAO's absence. Within regular staff meetings, leadership skills develop when the SSAO sets up an environment in which members can lead one another, support one another through solving problems and sharing experiences, and learn from one another's mistakes. This type of practice empowers growing professionals in their current role and for future leadership opportunities, and is a model of a high-impact practice in community college leadership.

Conclusion

The excellence perspective, when applied in every area of one's working life, can prove daunting and exhausting at times. Commitment to continuous improvement and exceeding standards and guidelines may lead one to wonder, "When is it okay to be just good enough?" The excellence perspective does not demand perfection; instead, it allows for rest, celebration, and appreciation. Vacation days, especially when classes are not in session, can revive, refresh, and bring new ideas to mind. Celebrating birthdays and holidays and major league sports victories bring people together to laugh and enjoy one another during the busy semester. Taking time to appreciate one another in the form of a thank you note or a coffee break adds a graceful touch to the workday filled with student needs. Resting, celebrating, and appreciating others merges with continuous improvement to produce artful results.

In conclusion, return to the Aristotelian concepts introduced at the beginning of the chapter: excellence is an art formed by habitually taking right actions that result in a virtuous outcome. Doing something and doing it well is the work of one committed to excellence, as Aristotle wrote and was translated by Sachs (2002) in *Nicomachean Ethics*, "…it belongs to a man of serious stature to do these things well and beautifully" (p. 11). The student affairs profession—alive and well in the community college—deserves and demands that the serious person do it well and beautifully.

References

ACPA—College Student Educators International & NASPA—Student Affairs Administrators in Higher Education (ACPA/NASPA). (2010). *Professional competency areas for student affairs practitioners*. Retrieved from http://www.naspa.org/images/uploads/main/Professional_Competencies.pdf

Astin, A. A., & antonio, a. l. (2012). *Assessment for excellence: The philosophy and practice of assessment and evaluation in higher education* (2nd ed.). Lanham, MD: Rowman & Littlefield.

Cloud, R. C. (2010). Epilogue: Change leadership and leadership development. In D. L. Wallin (Ed.), *New Directions for Community Colleges: No. 149. Leadership in an era of change* (pp. 73–79). San Francisco, CA: Jossey-Bass.

Council for the Advancement of Standards in Higher Education. (2012). *CAS professional standards for higher education* (8th ed.). Washington, DC: Author.

Durant, W. (1961). *The story of philosophy.* New York, NY: Pocket Books. (Original work published 1926)

Palomba, C. A., & Banta, T. W. (1999). *Assessment essentials: Planning, implementing and improving assessment in higher education.* San Francisco, CA: Jossey-Bass.

Peters, T. J., & Waterman, R. H. (1983). *In search of excellence: Lessons from America's best-run companies.* New York, NY: Harper Collins.

Rodkin, D. M. (2011). *Leadership competencies of community college senior student affairs officers in the United States* (Doctoral dissertation). Retrieved from ProQuest Dissertations and Theses database. (UMI No. 3496925)

Sachs, J. (2002). *Aristotle: Nicomachean ethics.* Newburyport, MA: Focus.

Thompson, C. (2013, April/May). Succession plan. *Community College Journal, 83*(5), 14–15.

Waple, J. N. (2006). An assessment of skills and competencies necessary for entry-level student affairs work. *NASPA Journal, 43*(1), 1–18.

ASHLEY KNIGHT *is the dean of Student Affairs at Harper College.*

NEW DIRECTIONS FOR COMMUNITY COLLEGES • DOI: 10.1002/cc

2

Recruitment, socialization, and development of new professionals are critical to the ongoing success, continuous improvement, and advancement of community colleges. The varied experiences and preparation of student services professionals create a complexity of needs that provide challenges to effectively and efficiently help them transition and flourish in their colleges. This chapter includes examples of effective practice in educating, transitioning, and developing new student affairs professionals, and implications for individuals, colleges, and graduate preparation faculty.

It Takes a Village: The Role of the Individual, Organization, and Profession in Preparing New Professionals

Christina J. Lunceford

Developing New Professionals

Community colleges are experiencing a historic shift in their personnel composition. Faculty and administrative leadership are retiring at rapid rates and many who were hired during a period of large growth within the community college sector, during the 1960s and 1970s, played a critical role in the development of their respective colleges and their success (Berry, Hammons, & Denny, 2001). While conversations on succession planning have primarily centered on community college leadership, there has been little emphasis on new student services professionals. New professionals play a critical role in the maintenance, advancement, and success of community colleges.

Student services professionals have backgrounds in many disciplines. In addition, the experiences and formal educational backgrounds of student services professionals at community colleges are typically much more varied than those at four-year colleges and universities. This range in preparation and training necessitates a formal process to socialize new professionals into their specific roles and positions, and also to the specific college and environment.

NEW DIRECTIONS FOR COMMUNITY COLLEGES, no. 166, Summer 2014 © 2014 Wiley Periodicals, Inc.
Published online in Wiley Online Library (wileyonlinelibrary.com) • DOI: 10.1002/cc.20097

Excellence in preparing new professionals in student affairs and services at community colleges involves making sure individuals are prepared to perform their professional roles and responsibilities to their full potential, have opportunities and support to continue to learn and develop as professionals and members of the organization, and are valued and able to participate fully as members of the organization. New professionals, supervisors, institutional leadership, and professional communities all have responsibilities in preparing new professionals; it is not the responsibility of a single role or position. Exploring excellence in preparing new professionals must include examining the role of formal education, prior experiences, socialization, and ongoing training and staff development.

Formal Education and Preparation

Where you work determines the minimum formal qualifications (e.g., diplomas, certificates, and degrees) for positions and what each individual is expected to know how to do. Community colleges typically have two different types of positions: academic positions and vocational positions. Each position and each college may require different qualifications to be considered for employment, which is determined at the district or college level. Entry-level professional student affairs positions are most often academic positions and many require a discipline-specific master's degree as a minimum qualification.[1] Even though a specific degree may be required for new professionals, the formal curriculum and experiential opportunities for each degree vary widely.

In spring 2012, Anne Hornak, Casey Ozaki, and I administered a survey to explore the nature of student affairs practice at community colleges (Lunceford, Ozaki, & Hornak, 2013). We focused on colleges in the Midwest region of the United States and received 171 completed surveys. Our survey participants indicated that on-the-job experience and institutional colleagues best prepared them for their work at their colleges (72% and 55%, respectively). Even though 72% of our participants had a master's degree, only 12.4% reported that their master's program did a "very good job" of preparing them to work at a community college. Higher education and student affairs graduate programs have an opportunity to play a large role in preparing new professionals for community colleges.

Some student affairs programs offer degrees and certificates specifically for community college practitioners. These programs may fill a certain niche in the market, especially for individuals currently working in community colleges who are looking to gain specific qualifications to increase opportunities for advancement and for individuals trying to break into highly competitive community colleges or districts. The same competition, however, does not exist across the entire United States. Although many student services professionals do not have degrees specifically in student affairs and services, student affairs graduate programs play a role in

NEW DIRECTIONS FOR COMMUNITY COLLEGES • DOI: 10.1002/cc

meeting the increased demand for master's degree level qualifications for new practitioners in community colleges and should be preparing individuals to work in all types of institutions.

Most formal graduate preparation programs have students explore the culture and characteristics of institutional types (e.g., public, private, two-year, four-year, and institutions that serve specific populations of students, such as historically Black colleges and universities, Hispanic-serving institutions, and women's colleges) and combinations of institutional characteristics in the core curriculum. In addition, most graduate programs have an experiential learning requirement in the form of practica, internships, fieldwork, or assistantships. However, graduate students are most often not immersed in environments long enough to fully understand what it is truly like to work in these specific environments.

Community colleges serve a large number of students of color, students living in poverty, and first-generation college students. It is up to each preparation program to determine how to best educate its students on how to work with individuals across difference and how to work within different types of institutions. Some graduate programs have courses specifically designed to understand difference and the nature of privilege and power from individual, group, organizational, and systems perspectives. Other programs are designed to embed diversity education throughout the curriculum. The level at which programs and individual course instructors are prepared and comfortable teaching about difference in terms of race, ethnicity, and income vary widely and may lead to a gap in preparing community college professionals.

Lessons From the Classroom.   I have taught courses in student affairs master's programs on diversity and multicultural competence in three programs in different regions of the United States. The courses served different purposes in the program curricula and varied in intended learning outcomes. Students read extensively, engaged in meaningful class discussions, and designed and sometimes implemented programs to help educate about or support marginalized or underrepresented populations. Yet, I felt there were still gaps in students' learning and understanding that I could address in a semester-long course.

Last semester I added a new assignment to a master's course I teach on multicultural competence in student affairs. I felt my students did not have a strong understanding of students outside a four-year residential university. Some of my students were first-generation college students, most had not had any experience with poverty, many were from strong high schools, and very few had ever been on a community college campus. I went to a training given at a few community colleges in our area titled Bridges out of Poverty (see Becker, Krodel, & Tucker, 2009) and decided to try something new.

I had students complete a community mapping project where they were assigned an inner-city high school or an urban or rural community college and had to identify neighborhood conditions, institutions, associations, businesses, and/or services that may influence a person's access to postsecondary education and messages received about education. Students worked in groups and met with educators at their assigned institution and mapped a certain mile radius for resources. This project allowed students to connect course material to an experiential learning opportunity and forced them to enter and really examine environments many of them have not ever seen. (Many indicated they had driven through similar areas, but never really looked at the environment.) In addition, even though not every group was assigned a community college, they were better able to understand how multiple forms of postsecondary education are effective and important in educating individuals and our citizenry.

Many of my students understood how community colleges may be used as a stepping stone for individuals to access four-year institutions; many of them did not, however, understand the multiple roles of the community college, the large clientele served, and best practices to work with the incredibly diverse student population. My students did not realize how little they really understood about how, particularly, race, ethnicity, and poverty influenced education and life experience. They also did not realize what it would be like to work at a community college or ever considered working at a community college. This changed for some after the assignment.

Socialization and Development of New Professionals

New professionals must understand the unique context of community colleges and their specific environment in order to be prepared fully for their positions. Watts and Hammons (2002) emphasized the importance of acclimating new professionals to the community college. They explored the history and context of professional development in community colleges and found that, while important, understanding advancements in technology and keeping up with public policy and societal demands was no longer enough to effectively develop staff. The new professional and the college have responsibilities for successful transition into the organization and specific unit.

A Model of Excellence.   This spring I had an opportunity to spend some time at William Rainey Harper College (Harper) to speak with those who work in student affairs and services (regardless of the formal title of the specific division in which they worked). I visited multiple colleges and what stood out to me at Harper was the overall excitement the staff had about their work—the innovative ideas and practices they presented, the support they espoused from the college leadership, and the collaborative nature of their work within student services and with teaching faculty. Harper was also one of the few colleges during my visits in which the professionals stated that they felt prepared for their positions (as much as was possible anyway, given the dynamic nature of community colleges) and seemed to be truly clear and confident in their work and knowledge about how the college operated and expectations for their roles and positions.

The New Counselor Training Program at Harper was recognized as an exemplary practice by the National Academic Advising Association (Joslin & Markee, 2011). In regards to training new student affairs professionals in this unit, the training program has four key components that make it a model program: (a) clear guidelines and expectations of roles and respon-sibilities, (b) sufficient time dedicated to training and socializing new pro-fessionals into their roles and the organization, (c) involvement of key indi-viduals, and (d) ongoing evaluation and professional development (Joslin & Markee, 2011; Otto, Rosenthal, & Kindle, 2013).

Guidelines and Expectations. The program has clearly stated history, learning goals and core competencies, and theoretical grounding of the role counselors play and the nature of their work with students. New staff members participate in an eight-week professional development program that covers expected attitudes for new staff members in regards to holis-tic development, in addition to knowledge and skills about their positions (Otto et al., 2013). The training has an informational component that in-cludes the more prescriptive elements of the work as an advisor (such as interpreting degree audits), a relational component (such as soft skills and important things to consider when working with individuals of various backgrounds), and a conceptual component primarily focused on student development and counseling. Individual units seldom have clearly artic-ulated public documents that incorporate each of these elements; these guidelines and expectations form the foundation for new staff training in this program.

Time Allocation and Commitment. As specified, the training program is designed for eight weeks. The training includes helping new profession-als understand the content and knowledge related to the informational, re-lational, and conceptual elements of the program, and also an experiential component that includes case studies, observations and practice, and home-work. The training is designed for each new professional and the timing in which one progresses depends on the preparation and previous training of each individual. If there are multiple individuals being trained, they receive the same core information but are reviewed separately. People in different roles participate in the training and review, and discuss the readiness of each individual to move to unsupervised practice.

Involvement of Key Individuals. Training new professionals is a col-laborative process that involves multiple individuals and roles within the immediate program and across the college. Harper reported that training is led by one counselor, but includes participation of roughly 15 other pro-fessionals (Joslin & Markee, 2011). Community college practitioners work with an incredibly diverse population, many with specific and unique needs. They also work in a rapidly changing environment that is influenced con-stantly and quickly by advancements in technology, and changes in internal and external policies and requirements. Introducing new professionals to personnel in multiple functional areas and in different positions through the college is crucial when they need to access information from other units to effectively support their students.

Ongoing Evaluation and Development.   Training and development of new professionals must continue throughout one's professional career. Reduced funding within community colleges has led to an increase in in-service training and in-house opportunities for professional development. Professionals within this program at Harper receive updates on informational, relational, and conceptual components each semester in a full-day in-service training. The unit also runs a regular brown bag training series. Finally, full- and part-time counselors both receive financial support for professional development.

The New Counselor Training Program at Harper is comprehensive, effective, and represents a program of excellence. Other components that are clearly documented are how the program is assessed, strengths from their perspective, and challenges. It is critical that colleges have comprehensive programs that allow for individual difference in preparation of new hires and effectively prepares and allows individuals to work effectively and efficiently. Comprehensive programs also allow individuals to be confident in their work, which leads to job satisfaction, increased staff retention, and less room for mistakes. Harper indicated that low incidence of mistakes in advising and working with students was the most crucial evidence they use to determine the quality of their New Counselor Training Program (Joslin & Markee, 2011).

Lessons From the Field.   As a faculty member and former student affairs administrator I have learned two critical lessons related to new professionals. First, it is important that individuals from different generations and levels of experience realize that everyone plays an important role within the organization. New professionals offer fresh ideas and perspectives to an organization, and more senior practitioners have a wealth of knowledge and information about the history and current practice; there must be mutual respect between the generations of staff members (Freeman & Taylor, 2009).

Second, ongoing training and professional development is critical to our work in student affairs and advancement of the professional and profession. Since the 1980s many practitioners have used the National Institute for Staff and Organization Development and the *Journal of Staff, Program, & Organization Development* for ideas and best practices in community colleges. ACPA—College Student Educators International and NASPA—Student Affairs Administrators in Higher Education are also two umbrella organizations that support practitioners. ACPA has two commissions that relate, specifically, to community college professionals: Commission for Student Development in the Two-Year College and Commission for Commuter Students and Adult Learners (see www.myacpa.org). NASPA has the

NEW DIRECTIONS FOR COMMUNITY COLLEGES • DOI: 10.1002/cc

Adult Learner and Students with Children Knowledge Community (see www.naspa.org). In-house leadership development programs may also be effective in helping individuals advance as professionals: not necessarily to change positions and take on more senior roles, but to be a leader in the profession, whatever the professional position.

Conclusion

The differences in preparation and training of new student affairs professionals emphasize the importance of creating effective ways to help new professionals transition into organizations and develop throughout their careers. Investments in new professionals in time and other resources will pay off in productivity, morale, innovation, and retention of staff and students. Community colleges serve a function within our education system that is often overlooked by student affairs as a profession and at the same time often the determining factor of further education and training for many underserved populations. As a profession, student affairs must work together to make sure individuals are prepared to help maintain and advance our work in community colleges.

Note

1. Individuals who do not have the specific degree listed in a job description may call the human resources department to explain how their different degree and experiences meet the minimum qualifications in order to move beyond the human resources screening phase of the hiring process.

References

Becker, K. A., Krodel, K. M., & Tucker, B. H. (2009). *Understanding and engaging under-resourced college students: A fresh look at the influence of economic class on teaching and learning in higher education.* Highlands, TX: aha! Process.

Berry, J. H., Hammons, J. O., & Denny, G. S. (2001). Faculty retirement turnover in community college: A real or imagined problem. *Community College Journal of Research and Practice, 25,* 123–136. doi:10.1080/10668920150218506

Freeman, J. P., & Taylor, C. (2009). Changing student characteristics and socialization. In A. Tull, J. B. Hurt, & S. A. Saunders (Eds.), *Becoming socialized in student affairs administration: A guidebook for new professionals and their supervisors* (pp. 67–88). Sterling, VA: Stylus.

Joslin, J. E., & Markee, N. L. (2011). *Academic advising administration: Essential knowledge and skills for the 21st century* [Monograph No. 22]. Manhattan, KS: NACADA.

Lunceford, C. J., Ozaki, C. C., & Hornak, A. M. (2013, March). *Developing student affairs practitioners at community colleges.* Paper presented at the annual conference of ACPA—College Student Educators International, Las Vegas, NV.

Otto, S., Rosenthal, E., & Kindle, J. L. (2013). William Rainey Harper College: Student advising through the life cycle. In T. O'Banion & W. G. Bumphus (Eds.), *Academic advising: The key to student success* (pp. 77–120). Washington, DC: Community College Press.

Watts, G. E., & Hammons, J. O. (2002). Professional development: Setting the context. In G. E. Watts (Ed.), *New Directions for Community Colleges: No. 120. Enhancing community colleges through professional development* (pp. 5–10). Hoboken, NJ: Wiley.

CHRISTINA J. LUNCEFORD *is an assistant professor of higher education and student affairs at Bowling Green State University.*

NEW DIRECTIONS FOR COMMUNITY COLLEGES • DOI: 10.1002/cc

3

The role of the mid-level manager as an organizer, communicator, and problem-solver in student affairs has been examined within the literature, but current discussion generally excludes the perspective of managers at community colleges. This chapter focuses on the importance of managerial identity and roles, particularly as it is enacted within a community college context. A framework is proposed as a tool for understanding the characteristics of the described managerial selves and how they are perceived by themselves and others.

Construction of the Mid-Level Management Position

Steve Tyrell

In any organization, mid-level managers serve in a critical role as conduits managing important tasks, roles, communications, and problems. The extent in student affairs that the mid-level manager's experience and perspective has been attended to by the student affairs profession is delimited to an organizational context that has largely excluded the community college perspective. As the profession continues to delve into the mid-level managerial experience, and with the proliferation of student housing, student leadership, and student civic engagement programs in the community college sector over the last decade, it is critical for all organizational participants in community colleges to understand the mid-level managerial position in student affairs and student services and how it must evolve with the challenges associated with the new growth in student life programs on their campuses.

Defining of the Managerial Self

The basis for understanding the mid-level manager position must include a clear definition of what the mid-level manager does in student affairs today and where there are degrees of differentiation between the community college sector and others in higher education. One definition of a manager is "A manager is the person responsible for planning and directing

NEW DIRECTIONS FOR COMMUNITY COLLEGES, no. 166, Summer 2014 © 2014 Wiley Periodicals, Inc.
Published online in Wiley Online Library (wileyonlinelibrary.com) • DOI: 10.1002/cc.20098

work of a group of individuals, monitoring their work, and taking corrective action when necessary..." (http://management.about.com/od /policiesandprocedures/g/manager1.htm). It captures many of the key elements of the individual juxtaposed between senior leaders and entry-level staff. In student affairs, these same key elements are also evident, but the positioning of the mid-level manager has been defined as "A mid-level manager in student affairs is a professional that reports to a senior student affairs officer (SSAO) or a person who directly reports to a SSAO and is responsible for the direction, control, and/or supervision of one or more student affairs functions or one or more professional staff member" (Tyrell & Farmer, 2006). This definition is nearly all-inclusive but still negates the possibility of a student affairs professional that is perceived mid-level in the organization by their peers, but does not fit this definition. At a prior campus, a Director of Multicultural Affairs reported to me as SSAO but did not have any professionals reporting to them. Everyone saw this individual as mid-level, and it reminds us that being managerial in how one's roles are defined, where the position sits in the midst of organizational tensions, and expectations set for the position can all contribute to being mid-level managerial in the absence of direct reports (or line) responsibilities. Thus, there is no one clear definition in student affairs of what is mid-level management. There is only agreement that SSAOs are not mid-level managers. Even the discussion of defining entry-level professionals is campus culture based and not clearly defined by the profession. Need we worry about the organizational relativism invoked in our deliberations of the construction of a definition? Probably not, because in essence, the construction of the managerial self (mid-level or otherwise) and one's ability to grasp the reality of exercising control over others may be more important than who fits the definition of mid-level manager.

The Construction of the Managerial Self

The construction of the managerial self has been well studied outside of higher education (Conrad, 1990; Foucault, 1983, 1991; Mumby, 1988; Smircich, 1985) but little has been added to this corpus of knowledge in the context of student affairs. The construction of the managerial self and its complement, the deconstruction of the managerial, allow us to understand how one develops as a mid-level manager. Why this is important: we need to understand how the managerial self is constructed if we are to fully grasp how the managerial self tenuously exercises control over others. The managerial self develops quietly over time through a host of formal training opportunities and informal experiences. The managerial self emerges over a long period of time through the accumulation of everyday experiences that the manager becomes "acculturated to." These acculturation experiences, sometimes overt and at other times, more sublime, are frames through

Table 3.1   Expectations of New, Mid, and Senior Mid-Level Managers

Expectations	New	Mid	Senior
+ Outlook by supervisor	Fresh ideas have arrived! Energy added to the organization	They know what they are doing; can accept new challenges	I readily rely heavily on them and see them as a peer
– Outlook by supervisor	Seems over-confident about knowledge competencies and skill sets	Worried they might be unchallenged	Are they burned out? Are they unwilling to try anything new?
+ Outlook of mid-level's self	Interested in learning and excited of new challenge	Confident I know my role and how to get things done with others	I could step into a major leadership role; are we able to assess our "effectiveness"?
– Outlook of mid-level's self	Worried I might not appear competent in all areas; will anyone listen to my ideas because I am new?	I wish I could just do my job and not be tasked with new assignments all the time	Is this it in my career? Can I offer more (elsewhere)? Why can't I "see" the vision?

Source: Tyrell (2010).

the self's interactions with others and less through isolated individual experiences.

The construction of the managerial self at any one point in time in one's managerial history is represented by a collection of socially/organizationally constructed identities and subjectivities. Examples of socially/organizationally constructed identities might include social constructs fixed in time, such as one's income status, age, student affairs functional area assignment, national organization membership, and philosophy on how best to support and challenge our students. Examples of one's managerial subjectivities are more fluid in nature and represent a collection of world views held about organizational approaches and views external to the organization and include managerial philosophies, such as "I treat everyone the same way" or "How I manage supervision is more situational in nature than consistent between employees" or "Social justice philosophies underpin how I interact with others in the organization."

As one's managerial self evolves over time, mid-level managers transition through phases regarding how they perceive their roles in their organization and often times, these perceptions are counterbalanced by the shifting perceptions held by their supervisors. Table 3.1 outlines three transitional phases for mid-level managers: new mid-levels who have been in their roles 0–3 years, mid mid-level managers who have been in their roles more than three years and no more than five years, and senior mid-level managers who have served in their roles more than five years.

As mid-level managers transition between their early years through their mid-career and finally into their senior years as mid-level managers in student affairs, mid-level managers reconstruct aspects of their identities and subjectivities. Their organizational and managerial world views transition as their managerial selves evolve (and not unlike the evolution of self that is often discussed outside of the context of the organizational self). How new, mid, and senior mid-levels come to define how a mid-level manager constructs and reconstructs his or her managerial self in the community college setting is critical. Years in the managerial role reflect how the community college professional may approach new challenges and demonstrate efficiency and effectiveness in the completion of tasks, and how they choose to exercise control over others. For example, the current emphasis for community college professionals to ramp up student completion efforts might be approached with excitement and apprehension. But a new mid-level manager's excitement and apprehension might be drawn from a very different worldview and identity context than one developed over time by a senior mid-level manager. Understanding the nuances associated with these transitional phases for the managerial self is essential to effectively planning professional development opportunities, whether formal or informal training or whether informal mentoring or professionalized coaching opportunities. We know that "expectations" and "apprehensions" described by supervisors and mid-levels at different transition points in their managerial careers can lead to all types of misreads and misunderstandings. These expectations and apprehensions can also lead to mid-levels gravitating to certain managerial roles in how they choose to work with others in the community college setting—something we will delve into further with the discussion of lone wolves, alliance keepers, and collaborative teams. These gravitational tugs and pulls are a result of the pressures mid-levels may feel in generating results and may through a sense of one's desire to either survive in the organization or be opportunistic in the organization (or both) begin to manifest a host of hidden agendas and unstated vested interests that results in the politicking of everyday work.

The Exercise of Unobtrusive Control in the Community College Setting

As the construction of the managerial self evolves over time (similar to the construction of the self), managers responsible for directing, planning, and controlling others engage in forms of control with others. The politics of everyday work is a discussion of exercising control over others to obtain desired results. Being a manager is about getting things done and getting people around you to do things for you. Managers have to exercise a certain amount of control as a necessity to get work done. Unobtrusive control occurs by getting people to *want to do* what you want them to do and/or controlling the managerial discourse/interaction in a manner that leads to the accomplishment of work.

Examples of unobtrusive control mechanisms (Tompkins & Cheney, 1985) in the community college work setting include how managers may choose to privilege access to information to some individuals and exclude others (Mumby & Clair, 1997); control the development of meeting agendas to include and exclude, to forefront certain topics and marginalize others; and engage in managerial discourse such as speech acts (remembering as a kid when the mother would ask "is the garbage full?" which the rational response "yes" was not the answer she was looking for but was a signal to take the garbage out of the house), use of implied solidarity (e.g., "we will be putting extra hours to complete this project this week" which translated into one or two of the group were really being told they were doing the work), and turn taking in managerial interactions that signals when a new topic is introduced and when a current topic comes to an end (as inferred by the shifts in turn taking by the manager).

As we bring these forms of unobtrusive forms of control to the forefront, we inadvertently paint a picture that one could infer as pseudocovert forms of manipulation. However, there is a tenuous nature to the exercise of managerial control where others resist these attempts and at times successfully effect a reversal (Foucault, 1983, p. 213). For example, think about those instances when you introduced a topic you wanted others to want to do and by the time you left the meeting, you realized that you are now doing the task yourself as a result of how the discourse unfolded. Community college managers are no different than other student affairs professionals in the sense that they are expected to get results from their staff and they are not expected to do so by using authoritative approaches. So managers and staff participate in a discursive dance where the outcomes are determined by the success of use of unobtrusive control mechanisms by managers and staff alike. In time, mid-level managers come to define their managerial identities and subjectivities as a result of the repetition of these control-mechanism-driven exchanges and yes, they also come to frame why mid-level managers transition through those three phases described earlier. But for the community college mid-level manager, the significance of the use of unobtrusive control mechanisms is not just instrumental in nature (i.e., the manager gets results), but that it plays itself out over and over again as the mid-level manager chooses to lead on completion of an action item in an institutional strategic plan, or designs an assessment process for a student learning outcomes study in their program, or how they choose to quickly respond to a student controversy. As the mid-level manager exercises control in these settings, others (e.g., student affairs professionals, students, student leaders, faculty, other administrative staff, trustees, alumni, and municipal leaders) become (sometimes semi-) cognizant of the layering of unobtrusive control mechanisms upon the topic at hand and whether they resist or agree to own the "task at hand," something seems to be lost as control is garnered and gained. As the pressures rise and remain to produce more and more organizational results with fewer and fewer resources, mid-level managers may feel compelled to use more and more unobtrusive control mechanisms to survive.

Lone Wolves, Alliance Keepers, and Collaborative Teams

Finally, the scale of effectiveness for mid-level managers is largely dependent on how they choose to exercise control in the conduit role in the organization. The conduit metaphor (Axley, 1984) asserts that the mid-level manager is centrally responsible for the movement of strategies and resource allocation up and down and back and forth across in the organization through communication strategies and including at times that unobtrusive control is natural in organizations. In the sometimes politicized environment of the community college setting, various mid-level roles emerge with the enactment of the conduit metaphor and thus managers move through these roles in order to accomplish work and forward goals for themselves and/or the organization.

We see these mid-level roles emerge as managers choose between enacting lone wolf strategies, protecting alliances created, and creating and sustaining collaborative teams. Managerial control is maintained as the community college professional shifts and slides between these arrangements.

For definitional purposes, the term team is defined here as any group of people organized to work together cooperatively to meet the needs of the organization by accomplishing a purpose and/or goal. The term collaboration is defined as involving parties who see different aspects of a problem. Gray (1989) wrote that collaborative teams engage in a process through which they constructively explore their differences and search for (and implement) solutions that go beyond their own limited vision of what is possible. Alliances are described as intraorganizational partnerships where the partners back each other, get work done quickly, protect their alliance-formed goals, and protect each other (and their areas) from potential organizational harm. Alliances are growing in higher education as more community college professionals are asked to do more with less. Collaborative arrangements, once cemented, can provide lasting and meaningful results in the organization, but they can take a lot of time to get to a point where these results are achieved. Alliances can protect elements of the status quo from others bent on implementing change, but once an alliance is known or exposed at the managerial level, others can resist alliance-related actions by working around them or over them (again, through the exercise of a reversal or other more overt means).

Lone wolves are effective at getting results quickly for senior leaders they serve, but those results tend to only last as long as the lone wolf

Table 3.2   Degrees of Teamness for Mid-Level Managers

Issue	Lone Wolves	Alliance Keepers	Collaborative Teams
Focus on hierarchy	Highly focused on delivering to both supervisor and supervisor's supervisor (=)	Only in respect to maintain position in organizational structure (=)	Not particularly focused on hierarchy except to the person who tasked the group (+)
Primary loyalty to	Supervisor (=)	Alliance members (=) Highly insulated (−)	Institution and each other (= /+)
Focus on stakeholders	Minimal focus, as they are loners (−)	Externals only viewed as either support or threat to alliance (−)	Interest is to get stakeholders' vested interests on table (+)
Time to accomplish task	Fast to complete task (+)	Moderate in short term of alliance (+)	Slow to complete task, unresponsive to market speed (−)
Receptive to change	Highly receptive! (+)	Less as time goes on; change in organization is OK if not a threat to alliance (−)	Can be very receptive if change seen as warranted to institution and group members (+)
Likeliness for change to last	Changes made discontinue when lone wolf leaves the organization (−)	Often irrelevant to alliances with long durations, sees most change as "passing fads to survive through" (=)	Greatest probability for change to last and be institutionalized as stakeholders take ownership for change (+)

Source: Tyrell (2010).

remains on the scene. Table 3.2 highlights the various pros and cons related to the enactment of these three managerial roles in the organization. One can readily denote the array of organizational tensions present as mid-level managers transition between these roles.

As community college professionals debate, launch, and lament how best to move their agendas forward at their institutions, the frequency of enacting one or two of these three managerial roles over the other tends to over time create new descriptions of how the manager sees themselves in the organization coupled with how staff who work for the manager perceive them. Four new descriptive managerial roles emerged for managers who engaged in long-term lone wolf, alliance keeper, and collaborative team

Table 3.3   Outcomes of Teamwork: Task Accomplishment x Group Satisfaction

	Members of the Groups Satisfied	Members of the Group Dissatisfied
Tendency to Get Task Accomplished	Champion (seen as collaborative-based) Forwards collective group's interests to others; seen as deliberate by collaborative-minded participants; interested in finding solutions that are based upon group weighing all vested interests and work toward a group decision where as many members own the solution as they own the problem.	Despot (seen as alliance- or lone-wolf-based) Forwards one's interests past group's interests; unable to recognize other's interests; see as "go-getter" from above but despised by peers and subordinates; may trample over others feelings, roles, and rules in group settings. Has little ownership for the group's solution unless it matches individual or alliance's needs. Task accomplished is situated in terms of despot's expectations— uncollaborative outcome results . . .
Tendency to Not Get Task Done	Protector (seen as alliance- or departmental-based) Protects alliance or own department's interests and attempts to *position/replace these over* collective group's interests, seen as the "make it go away" person; seen as champion of the status quo, seen as highly effective by subordinates and allied colleagues and difficult to work with by others. May try to derail or redirect group's work to protect department's and/or alliance's needs.	Exile (seen as alliance-, departmental- or lone-wolf-based) Disengaged though present—fails to share vested interests with group; seen as ineffective by others; may feel that no one sees their (or their department's) worth. Does not volunteer to assist in getting task done. Has no ownership in group's decision.

Source: Tyrell (2010).

behaviors. These new roles are *champions, despots, protectors,* and *exiles.* These four roles vary from each other depending on the manager's ability to achieve results and the level of the subordinates' satisfaction with group goals and achievement of departmental tasks. Managers are typified into one of these four roles and are possibly even celebrated or vilified by their staff and themselves. Table 3.3 highlights the characteristics of these constructed managerial selves, and how they are perceived by themselves and others.

We know that these constructed managerial selves are not fixed in time. We also know that at times, some longer term managers will shift among these four roles with themselves and how they are perceived by their staff. Again, these roles emerge through the construction of the managerial self, the exercise of unobtrusive control, and the gravitational pull to get results through the shift between one of three team approaches described above.

The question that remains for mid-level managers is not which role you have assumed today, but more so, how do we challenge each other to query where the presence of lone wolves, alliance keepers, collaborators, exiles, champions, despots, and protectors are in our midst? How are their behaviors benefitting and holding back our ability to support and challenge our students? Allow us to achieve our professional goals? Our institutional obligations and goals?

How can we best open up the organizational conversation to acknowledge where information has been privileged? Where implied solidarity detracts from transparent communication? Where we manage meaning in interactions that results in others becoming marginalized and/or silenced? These questions are lying below the surface of everyday interactions between managers and others. The point of raising these questions is not to apologize for how these behaviors unfold, how unobtrusive control gets enacted, or how managerial roles become temporarily reified in time. The point for the community college professional to become effective in recognizing how they enact these behaviors in interactions with others. And more importantly to recognize in time, only they can choose what form and function of their managerial identity and subjectivity will come to define who they are in the student affairs organization and how their managerial selves come to describe how they present themselves and the purpose of their work with others. The politics of everyday work in the student affairs organization will be ever present as long as two or more professionals choose to interact with each other. But there is a belief that the range of transparency in these interactions can be expanded when and where mid-levels best come to understand how their interactions with others come to describe the managerial self they have constructed for themselves.

As student affairs professionals rise into role of middle management, they have been or will become acculturated to ascribe to a number of managerial roles described here for a variety of reasons. Some will shift between roles as an instrumental function of getting the task done for the organization. Some will acclimate to certain managerial roles due to their own histories that they bring to the mid-level managerial role. And many may take on roles that transition between what is needed for task achievement and what histories they bring to the table. What may be important as a first step for student affairs professionals is to understand what managerial roles you enact in everyday work and interactions with others. However, the more important point may be why you chose to enact a particular role or set of roles and what roles will you choose to enact in the future?

As we move in and through various managerial roles, we form for any moment in time a managerial identity. Over time, this identity shapes and reshapes as a result of forces from without and within the manager's organizational values. To some degree, the identity construct is more fluid than static and fixed (each for any moment in time). But for mid-level managers, it is critical that we become fully cognizant of how one's managerial identity formulates and reformulates over time. They need to become particularly aware of how they come to understand their own organizational identity as they exercise control over others and why that identity exerts itself in some instances, wanes in others, and is recast again. Without maintaining a certain degree of vigilance on the roles we assume and replicate, we run the risk that our managerial identity can fade into the gestalt of our self-create organizational landscape. Years later, we can be then left with running the risk of wondering how we became who we are in our organizational life. As critical organizational participants, if we continually inspect our use of everyday discourse to accomplish our work with others, especially when we choose to exercise control unobtrusively or otherwise, eventually we will create a new space in organizational talk where a more transparent dialogue will exist regarding the agency attached to the managerial roles we enact with others.

References

Axley, S. (1984). Managerial and organizational communication in terms of the conduit metaphor. *Academy of Management Review, 9*, 428–437.

Conrad, C. (1990). *Strategic organizational communication: An integrated perspective* (2nd ed.). Fort Worth, TX: Holt, Rinehart, and Winston.

Foucault, M. (1983). Why study power: The question of the subject. In H. Dreyfus & P. Rabinow (Eds.), *Michel Foucault: Beyond structuralism and hermeneutics* (pp. 208–216). Chicago, IL: University of Chicago Press.

Foucault, M. (1991). Governmentality. In G. Burchell, C. Gordon, & P. Miller (Eds.), *The Foucault effect: Studies of governmentality* (pp. 8–104). Chicago, IL: University of Chicago Press.

Gray, B. (1989). *Collaborating: Finding common ground for multiparty problems.* San Francisco, CA: Jossey-Bass.

Mumby, D. (1988). *Communication and power in organizations: Discourse, ideology and domination.* Norwood, NJ: Ablex Publishing.

Mumby, D., & Clair, R. (1997). Organizational discourse. In T. A. van Dijk (Ed.), *Discourse as social interaction* (pp. 181–205). Thousand Oaks, CA: Sage.

Smircich, L. (1985). Is organizational culture a paradigm for understanding organizations and ourselves? In P. J. Frost, L. F. Moore, M. R. Louis, C. C. Lundberg, & J. Martin (Eds.), *Organizational culture* (pp. 55–72). Beverly Hills, CA: Sage.

Tompkins, P. K., & Cheney, G. (1985). Communication and unobtrusive control in contemporary organizations. In R. D. McPhee & P. K. Tompkins (Eds.), *Organizational communication: Traditional themes and new directions* (pp. 179–210). Newbury Park, CA: Sage.

Tyrell, S. (2010, March). *The politics of everyday work for the mid-level manager: Teamwork, alliances & discourse.* Paper presented to University of Akron, Akron, OH.

Tyrell, S., & Farmer, M. (2006, March). *A comparative analysis of mid-level managers' (and other staff in student affairs) skills and knowledge competencies.* Paper presented for the Mid Level Research Team, Commission on Administration Leadership, ACPA Convention, Indianapolis, IN.

STEVE TYRELL *is the president of North Country Community College.*

NEW DIRECTIONS FOR COMMUNITY COLLEGES • DOI: 10.1002/cc

4

The unique nature and mission of community colleges directly shapes the role and function of a senior student affairs officer (SSAO). Broadly, the community college mission is shaped by a vision of fulfilling several commitments to local communities. This includes admitting all applicants through an open access admissions policy and providing comprehensive educational programs leading to associate's degrees, career and technical education, basic skills education, certificates, and the transfer pathway to baccalaureate-granting institutions, as well as lifelong learning courses. This chapter will discuss the role of the SSAO within a community college organizational structure. Career paths will be explored including competencies needed in this role. Implications include promising practices for aspiring SSAOs as well as recommendations for search committees who must no longer neglect SSAOs as potential presidents.

The Role of the Executive-Level Student Services Officer Within a Community College Organizational Structure

John Hernandez, Ignacio Hernández

Executive-level student services officers in community colleges are unique because of the students they serve and the mission of their institutions. When compared to their peers in baccalaureate granting institutions, research shows that community colleges students are more likely to be female, racial minorities, older, from lower income families, and attend part-time (Provasnik & Planty, 2008). Students in community colleges can choose from an array of educational programs in a wide range of disciplines.

Each community college has one executive-level student affairs officer although specific job titles may vary; the positions are most commonly referred to as chief student services officer (CSSO) or senior student affairs officer (SSAO). The American Association of Community Colleges (AACC) offers a glimpse into the demographic characteristics of executive and managerial staff at community colleges around the country. AACC's estimates on gender and race of community college executive and managerial employees indicate that 53% are female and 80% are White (AACC, 2013a). Executive diversity is a necessary goal for all student affairs organizational structures given the broad range of students, staff, and faculty that comprise today's community college campuses.

In general, this executive position functions within the organizational structure and is responsible for meeting the multifaceted needs of students and the various student services offices and departments across the institution. Most SSAOs hold a position on the president's cabinet and are responsible for the overall assessment, planning, coordination, delivery, funding, and evaluation of all student services and programs. As integral members of the executive leadership team and stakeholders in the development of institutional policies, SSAOs are responsible for leading shared governance initiatives with various constituents. SSAOs work to enact the mission while striving to achieve the vision of the college. SSAOs must effectively manage fiscal and human resources while also taking a leadership role in advancement and fundraising efforts.

The role of an SSAO in a community college is quite fluid and may vary from campus to campus depending on localized needs and demands. In exploring the scope of the work of an SSAO in a community college, it is necessary to understand the context of community colleges in which student affairs work is situated.

The Unique Context of Student Affairs Practice in Community Colleges

One instance of the variation in the role of the SSAO is the case of a smaller community college. A modestly sized campus may rely on the SSAO to "wear several hats" where they are responsible for a diverse portfolio of reporting units and departments. The SSAOs may also take on responsibilities and roles that are more operational in focus. For example, the SSAO in these colleges may be the administrator responsible for adjudicating student discipline, while overseeing areas traditionally not housed in student services, such as auxiliary services. The scope of their day-to-day work may mirror those of a dean or associate vice president at larger institutions.

Most community colleges, however, regardless of enrollment numbers, place a great deal of emphasis on establishing and maintaining relationships with external constituents and local community organizations. Given this expectation, an SSAO is very likely to be active in the local chamber of commerce as well other civic organizations. The SSAO may also be expected to play a key role in K–12 education and/or workforce development partnerships for local community needs.

An SSAO plays an integral role in student success and community college students benefit greatly from transition programs into campus life as well the academic expectations of higher education (Jalomo, 2001). Given their role and potential to impact positive student outcomes, it is common for the SSAO to be an active participant in campus-wide core committees. This level of involvement allows the SSAO to provide recommendations to the president or to help shape the overall operation of the institution. Recommendations may impact fiscal operations, facilities management, strategic planning, technology, and outcomes assessment. Additionally, it is quite common for an SSAO to be an integral member of an institutional accreditation committee and to play a key role in the self-evaluation process particularly in student support program standards.

In multicampus community college districts, SSAOs may see their involvement increasing significantly in the number and scope of committees served. The nature of a multicampus district necessitates participation in district-level meetings and collaborations with fellow SSAOs from sister campuses. This level of participation and collaboration requires additional layers of interface and coordination with other campuses or with a centralized district structure.

Competencies, Traits, and Skills Needed for Senior-Level Student Affairs Positions

The community college SSAOs should be able to assess opportunities for teaching and learning at all levels of their division. Sandeen (1991) listed three roles where an SSAO must demonstrate personal competence: manager, mediator, and educator. Similarly, Saunders and Cooper (1999) identified personnel management and leadership skills, such as resolving conflict, building effective teams, collaborating with others, implementing effective decisions, influencing others, and understanding organizational behavior, as desirable skills for aspiring executive-level student service officers. Organizations for community college professionals offer tangible frameworks for community college leaders aspiring to executive-level positions. Since 2005, the AACC has championed their listing of competencies for current and aspiring leaders. These competencies were mostly directed toward presidents; however, SSAOs may also benefit from the guidelines proffered by AACC. Recently, AACC released a second edition of competencies for community college leaders with a process-oriented framework for emerging leaders (AACC, 2013b).

Professional organizations, such as AACC, ACPA—College Student Educators International, and NASPA—Student Affairs Administrators in Higher Education each sponsor and support various institutes and professional development opportunities for aspiring and current SSAOs. Additionally, ACPA and NASPA collaborated to develop a set of 10 professional competencies as a self-assessment tool to identify the skills needed within the student affairs profession (ACPA/NASPA, 2010). The competencies most relevant to an SSAO role include assessment, evaluation and research, human and organizational resources, law, policy and governance, and leadership.

Career Paths to the Senior-Level Student Affairs Position

Much of the research literature on career pathways for community college leaders focuses on the presidency (see Amey & VanDerLinden, 2002; Eddy, 2010). Aspiring senior-level student affairs officers in community colleges are likely aware that leadership takes many forms. Similarly, multiple individuals with a variety of job titles and responsibilities often enact their own leadership in community colleges. For those individuals committed to student affairs and the student affairs profession, the role of the SSAO is likely to be an enticing career goal. Sitting SSAOs will most likely report heterogeneous career pathways and their roles and responsibilities require a high level of competency and skill in many domains. Biddix (2013) cited a limited number of studies to have explored the career paths to the senior-level student affairs position. These authors stated that between 1983 and 2012 only five studies had been published on the topic. Limited research and multiple career pathways suggest that there is no consensus about a consistent pathway to an SSAO position. Most recently, Biddix (2013) described which type of positions or level of experience most often lead to SSAO positions while alluding to how pathways may differ between institutional types in higher education. The research on career pathways has typically examined SSAOs' job titles in reverse chronological order ending with graduate degree completion (Biddix, 2013; Renn, 2004).

In community colleges, it is not uncommon for a SSAO to come from administrative areas, such as admissions and records, financial aid, or counseling. Career paths to an SSAO position may follow a traditional trajectory from entry level, to middle management, to senior level. While this process is typically marked by advancement from a director or dean position to the SSAO role, there are some slightly divergent pathways (Biddix, 2013). For professionals considering a senior-level position, it is important to note that titles are not always reflective of the scope and depth of work, level of responsibility, or the functional areas or programs under one's portfolio. These will vary depending on the size and type of community college. Thus, it is often more about the specific set of experiences a candidate has acquired rather than the title of their previous role(s).

Educational attainment is an important consideration for those considering a senior-level student affairs position. Administrative and senior-level positions in higher education deem a master's or doctoral degree indispensable for upward career mobility (Amey, VanDerLinden, & Brown, 2002; Davis, 2003; Saunders & Cooper, 1999). A cursory review of SSAO job postings in community colleges would likely show that a doctoral degree is preferred, but not required. With finite SSAO positions, advanced degrees or certificates may help applicants' chances in being considered for a senior-level job. Nonetheless, it may also be true that an advanced degree or additional professional development may be necessary simply to maintain a current position within a community college organizational structure.

Career advancement and mobility for aspiring and current SSAOs often involve decisions related to remaining in the same institution. Staying in their current colleges may stem from a potential to advance while being mobile and changing positions or institutions may be necessary in order for a vertical career move. Either way, a community college SSAO will likely have to carefully calculate when the time comes for an institutional change. In their research, Amey and VanDerLinden (2002) reported an overwhelming 70% of SSAOs were employed at the same community college for 10 years or more. Additionally, the same study reported 62% of SSAOs were in their immediate previous positions for less than five years, while another 67% also stayed in their second previous position for less than five years. These moves may stem from potential advancement opportunities and balancing the timing of being mobile by changing positions or institutions in order for a vertical career move.

Reflection of a Current SSAO: John

Completing my ninth year of my first role as SSAO, I can evaluate the skill sets needed to be effective in this position and how those continue to refine themselves over time. Many of the attributes that have assisted me are not unique to the role but allow me to navigate this role effectively. For example, building relationships based on trust and good will; the ability to multitask while moving in and out of multiple roles at any given moment; advanced organizational skills that allow me to access, monitor, and follow through with a high volume of information and details, and knowing under what circumstances to process this information as a generalist or a specialist; and an ability to advocate for needs of students and the full array of resources needed to provide these critical services.

In an age of greater accountability to external stakeholders (e.g., legislators and accrediting commissions) and to student success reforms across the nation, the SSAO has become an integral institutional representative. SSAOs must now "tell our story" to external constituents while also serving as a "bridge" that facilitates dialogue on our campuses on critical national issues (i.e., student success scorecards, student learning outcomes assessment, data-driven decision making, performance-based funding, etc.). Additional experiences expected of SSAOs include the ability to develop a framework for ongoing outcomes assessment and evaluating institutional effectiveness, fundraising and advancement, enrollment management and projecting enrollment trends, as well as collective bargaining and negotiation skills. I have also gained valuable exposure and experience through my participation in association with volunteer leadership roles. I have been an active member in one such professional association, ACPA—College

Student Educators International, and as an SSAO currently serve on the governing board as member-at-large representing senior-level student affairs officers. The benefits of this type of involvement are multiple and increase my capacity to network with a community of colleagues across the country in addressing common issues and national trends that increase my understanding and awareness of how these impact the local work at my institution.

Additionally, I believe there is an expectation in our profession to give back to the next generation of senior practitioners and to that end I have served on the faculty of institutes that aim to reach mid-level professionals and another for aspiring SSAOs. It is not uncommon for SSAOs to teach or be guest lecturers at local graduate preparation programs or to serve on their advisory boards; to present at regional or national conferences; to be interviewed by graduate students for class presentations or papers; to publish articles in local or national journals, newsletters, and related periodicals; and certainly to mentor and guide those aspiring to our roles.

Conclusion

Professionals considering a career move into a SSAO position in a community college should be well aware of the institutional context and students they will serve entering the position. The historic mission of community colleges has called for local impact while accepting all students. While every community college's administrative structure can vary, it is likely that only one individual holds the senior-level student affairs position. Localized needs and institutional variation may impact student affairs practice. Individuals considering career moves may want to spend adequate time assessing if their values are a good fit with the mission and vision of the college. This sense-making process can involve participation in organizations, such as AACC, ACPA, and NASPA. Each organization offers guiding frameworks for professional practice in community colleges and student affairs, which take the form of publications, leadership institutes, and annual conferences.

The research literature on career pathways for SSAOs in community colleges is sparse but there are some common themes worth considering. First, it is important to understand there is no one way for individuals to ascend to a senior-level student affairs position. Career pathways are highly individualized and dependent on contextual factors. Second, the positive impact of graduate education is evident in examining career pathways. Master's and doctoral degrees are very likely to be requisite achievements for candidates seeking to lead a community college's division of student affairs. Finally, an SSAO position may not be a role for everyone. The demands and expectations of the job are high and for many professionals it can be the culmination of a successful career while for others it serves as a springboard for presidencies and other related executive positions.

References

ACPA—College Student Educators International & NASPA—Student Affairs Administrators in Higher Education (ACPA/NASPA). (2010). *Professional competency areas for student affairs practitioners.* Washington, DC: Authors.

American Association of Community Colleges (AACC). (2005). *Competencies for community college leaders.* Washington, DC: Author. Retrieved from http://www.aacc.nche.edu/Resources/competencies/Pages/partc.aspx

American Association of Community Colleges (AACC). (2013a). *Staff employment distribution.* Washington, DC: Author. Retrieved from http://www.aacc.nche.edu/AboutCC/Trends/Pages/staffemploymentdistribution.aspx

American Association of Community Colleges (AACC). (2013b). *Competencies for community college leaders* (2nd ed.). Washington, DC: Author. Retrieved from http://www.aacc.nche.edu/newsevents/Events/leadershipsuite/Pages/competencies.aspx

Amey, M. J., & VanDerLinden, K. E. (2002). *Career paths for community college leaders.* (Research Brief Leadership Series, No. 2, AACC-RB-02-2). Washington, DC: American Association of Community Colleges.

Amey, M. J., VanDerLinden, K. E., & Brown, D. F. (2002). Perspectives on community college leadership: Twenty years in the making. *Community College Journal of Research and Practice, 26*(7/8), 573–589.

Biddix, J. P. (2013). Directors, deans, doctors, divergers: The four career paths of SSAOs. *Journal of College Student Development, 54*(3), 315–321.

Davis, J. R. (2003). *Learning to lead: A handbook for postsecondary administrators.* (ACE/Praeger Series in Higher Education). Lanham, MD: Rowman & Littlefield.

Eddy, P. L. (2010). *Community college leadership: A multidimensional model for leading change.* Sterling, VA: Stylus.

Jalomo, R., Jr. (2001). Institutional policies that promote persistence among first-year community college students. In B. K. Townsend & S. B. Twombly (Eds.), *Community colleges: Policy in the future context* (pp. 261–282). Westport, CT: Ablex.

Provasnik, S., & Planty, M. (2008). *Community colleges: Special supplement to The Condition of Education 2008* (NCES 2008-033). Washington, DC: National Center for Education Statistics, Institute of Education Sciences, U.S. Department of Education.

Renn, K. (2004). Introduction. In K. Renn & C. Hughes (Eds.), *Roads taken: Women in student affairs at mid-career* (pp. 173–180). Sterling, VA: Stylus.

Sandeen, A. (1991). *The chief student affairs officer: Leader, manager, mediator, educator.* San Francisco, CA: Jossey-Bass.

Saunders, S. A., & Cooper, D. L. (1999). The doctorate in student affairs: Essential skills and competencies for midmanagement. *Journal of College Student Development, 40,* 185–191.

JOHN HERNANDEZ *is the vice president of student services at Santiago Canyon College.*

IGNACIO HERNÁNDEZ *is an assistant professor of educational leadership at California State University, Fresno.*

5

This chapter explores CAS as a tool for collecting assessment and evaluation data in community college student affairs offices. Details are provided about accessing the self-assessment modules, as well as the resources available to assist colleges with data collection. Finally, the chapter will explore how to use the data to advocate for programming, and the implementation of findings to leverage resources for future work.

An Overview of CAS Standards: The Role in Self-Assessment and Evaluation

Anne M. Hornak

The Council for the Advancement of Standards in Higher Education (CAS, 2012) promotes standards within student affairs to encourage professionals to develop programs and services that are consistently incorporating student learning and development into the mission. While CAS is not a formal accreditation agency and does not purport to enforce accreditation, it is a professional member organization that provides guidance regarding standards in student affairs work (CAS, 2012) and is used to guide curriculum for higher education, educational leadership, and student affairs graduate preparation programs across the United States.

History of CAS

CAS was established in 1979 as the Council for the Advancement of Standards in Student Services/Development Programs, later to emerge as the Council for the Advancement of Standards in Higher Education. Prior to 1979, other similar organizations emerged and quickly dissolved as a result of political tensions and member dissatisfaction. The emergence and solvency of CAS was a direct answer to the need for an organization that was less political and more focused on work establishing standards and platforms directly addressing the values and interests of student affairs professionals. The standards provide criteria to evaluate the quality and effectiveness of programs within student affairs and development. As the profession of student affairs grew, so did the need for quality standards to

New Directions for Community Colleges, no. 166, Summer 2014 © 2014 Wiley Periodicals, Inc.
Published online in Wiley Online Library (wileyonlinelibrary.com) • DOI: 10.1002/cc.20100

inform practice and preparation (CAS, 2012). It is critical to state that CAS is not a formal accrediting agency; rather it is a member consortium of over 40 higher education professional associations, contributing to a level of rigor and credibility to the self-assessment process.

The landscape of higher education and student affairs/services has changed over the last 34 years, as well as the mission of CAS. In 2008, CAS established a new mission statement:

> The mission of the Council for the Advancement of Standards in Higher Education (CAS) is to promote the improvement of programs and services to enhance the quality of student learning and development. CAS is a consortium of professional associations who work collaboratively to develop and promulgate standards and guidelines and to encourage self-assessment (CAS, 2008, para. 2).

The new mission statement represents the changing nature of student affairs work related to student learning and development. To fully understand and embrace the role and scope of CAS in the landscape of higher education, it is important to look at the depth of representation across the member professional associations. The membership represents every functional area within student affairs and services, as well institutional type.

CAS Standards

The CAS standards have undergone many revisions as higher education has changed. The latest revisions reduced 14 standards to 12, by integrating several elements. In addition, the pervasiveness of technology and distance learning has influenced revisions and the need to address learning outcomes through technology. The 12 standards are: mission; program; organization and leadership; human resources; ethics; law, policy, and governance; diversity, equity, and access; institutional and external relations; financial resources; technology; facilities and equipment; and assessment and evaluation. Embedded within the standards are specified learning outcome domains which place an emphasis on specific observable student behaviors that practitioners can use to judge learning and development achievement. The 2002 revision of the general standards includes a table listing the 16 domains with examples of achievement indicators. The 2002 revision and the current revision (2012) recognize the potential impact of educational programming and reinforce the importance that programs consider student learning their primary mission (CAS, 2012). Additionally, in 2006 CAS published the *Frameworks for Assessing Learning and Development Outcomes* (Strayhorn, 2006) to provide further clarity and guidance in developing activities to reinforce learning.

NEW DIRECTIONS FOR COMMUNITY COLLEGES • DOI: 10.1002/cc

CAS in Use

The use of the CAS standards as a tool to develop high-quality programs is an internally driven activity. The motivation and desire to conduct a programmatic self-assessment is often driven by institutional demands; however, CAS maintains that internally driven regulation is more desirable than externally demanded assessment because individuals within the community college know their programs, missions, and goals the best. The tools and resources needed for executing a thorough evaluation of programs can be extensive; however, the information obtained can be tremendously informative in practice.

Community college student affairs and services are unique in that many offices and programs are understaffed and professionals are cross-trained to serve the needs of diverse students (Tull, Hirt, & Saunders, 2009). This role is distinct in that they need to be prepared to respond to societal changes quickly to remain current and relevant in their communities (Helfgot, 2005).

Many community colleges struggle to identify concrete examples that use CAS as a tool in the assessment process. An exemplary case comes from William Rainey Harper College in Illinois where CAS is used in their internal program review process. The student activities department used the CAS standards as the foundation for an examination of the current state of the program. The goal of the office is "to create quality campus activity programs that are engaging, developmental, and experiential. This goal is in direct alignment with the Council for the Advancement of Standards... [Student activity self assessment guide]" (A. Knight, personal communication, January 8, 2013). In evaluating the goals and objectives, data were collected that assessed educational opportunities, offered by the department that extend beyond the classroom. The review found that the program is effective in offering programing and activities related to multicultural development, leadership, social and recreational activities, as well as special interest programs and services.

As a constantly evolving and changing institution, the need for quality assessment and evaluation data is critical. Decisions about quality programs and services must be based on solid assessment and outcomes data. Using the CAS self-assessment guides (SAGs) to assess and evaluate programs provides reliable data that can be used to leverage resources, both fiscal and human. The role of how institutions use CAS varies and is not prescribed by the organization. The SAGs can be used to design new programs and services, to assess how programs are performing, for staff development, and as part of an institutional self-study. The remainder of this chapter will explore using the SAGs as part of an institutional self-study.

CAS Self-Assessment Guides

CAS provides a self-assessment guide for each standard, which includes a comprehensive process for program evaluation. There are seven steps to implement the guides in a self-study. The first step is establishing and preparing the self-assessment team. This involves determining which functional areas will be evaluated. The recommendation would be to look across the college and establish a cycle for the functional areas that offset one another. Conducting a comprehensive and in-depth self-study can be a tremendous task; however if the cycle can also match an external accreditation or internal program review, time and effort are maximized. These initial planning stages should include the full staff, including support staff, faculty, and representative students, with the goal of shared ownership and voice in the evaluation process. This process should also include team training and establishing the specific guidelines for the study, for example, which standards will be assessed during the study.

The next step is initiating the self-study. During this step, team members rate the criterion measures individually and then discuss collectively how well the program meets the criteria. CAS provides rating scales within the SAGs that reflect the goals and essence of each standard.

The next step in the self-study process is to identify and summarize evaluative evidence. This is one of the most important steps in the process of the study. Merely identifying the strengths and weaknesses of programs and functional areas is not enough depth to judge program merits. The qualitative and quantitative data should be viewed as documentation to support and validate the CAS team member's findings. The data are used to further develop and refine learning outcomes and goals. The findings should also provide an opportunity for the larger college community to interpret the meaning of the findings and provide comment, which may result in alternative interpretations of the study results.

Next, the study team will identify discrepancies from their rankings and interpretations of the findings. This step is critical as team members review each criterion measure that states not done, unsatisfactory, or cases where other rated discrepancies of two or more are noted. For each discrepancy and shortcoming identified a specific rationale is prepared to address a resolution plan. Discrepancies are usually found between assessment criteria and actual practice at the college. A resolution plan should identify how a new practice will be implemented to resolve the issue.

Following the identification of discrepancies, the next step is to determine appropriate corrective action. This step is critical to validate the process and make the essential changes that team is recommending. This is often the step where departments, offices, and functional areas do not follow through because the corrections that need to be made seem overwhelming. It is essential to divide up the overall task into manageable steps

NEW DIRECTIONS FOR COMMUNITY COLLEGES • DOI: 10.1002/cc

and develop a step-by-step plan. Additionally, setting priorities for change can help facilitate and ensure the changes are made.

Recommending special action for program enhancement is the next step in the self-study process. During the study, team members may find programs that are of good quality and meet the criteria established in the rankings. However, unless team members are satisfied with meeting basic standards, many self-studies find opportunities for program enhancement. The goal of the self-study is to promote gold standards and excellence in programs and practice. Finding ways for program enhancement is as critical as addressing the known weaknesses and program shortcomings.

The final step in the use of SAGs is to prepare an action plan. The action plan is what will set all the findings in motion and operationalize the future direction of the program. The process for preparing the final action plan involves how the program changes will be implemented, identifying resources for the changes, establishing dates for completion of the action plan steps, as well as identifying who is responsible for completion of the steps, and finally setting up the tentative schedule for follow up self-studies. During this implementation step, it is critical to establish ongoing data collection. The first self-study is the most challenging for a college; the follow up studies should be easier as the data collection procedures have been established. Additionally, the amount of data may not be as onerous if a well-established ongoing data collection process is established.

Importance of CAS

The process and procedures for conducting a self-guided programmatic study has been outlined in this chapter. The importance of a self-study cannot be underscored. Student affairs and services are often seen as disposable elements in higher education; therefore having data to provide validity to the services being offered can give a unit credibility. The academic units often are established as the primary vehicle for student learning and development. However, the cocurricular value of student affairs at a community college cannot be overlooked. Functional areas with high-quality, gold standard programs are highly valued to executive-level leaders. It is critical that self-study team leaders create a culture of assessment and evaluation. The self-study can be the springboard to an ongoing process of data collection and program refinement. In writing this chapter, I tried to find examples from community colleges that are actively using CAS in their assessment processes. The data are not readily available, which reinforces the commitment it takes to conduct an extensive, ongoing CAS assessment. The CAS website and other professional organizations provide some information and resources to conduct a study; however, as a learning community we need to find ways to provide resources to aid colleges.

Conclusion

In conclusion, the underlying goal of the CAS standards is to promote quality student learning and development. Quality should be the minimum goal, the ultimate goal of standards and guidelines is to move closer to excellence, defined as the consistent application of the kinds of actions termed best or promising practices. Higher education and community colleges are consistently reinventing themselves to meet the internal and external needs of their communities. It is critical that revisioning is done through a consistent and standard frame of practice.

References

Council for the Advancement of Standards in Higher Education (CAS). (2008). *CAS mission*. Retrieved from http://www.cas.edu/mission

Council for the Advancement of Standards in Higher Education (CAS). (2012). *CAS professional standards for higher education* (8th ed.). Washington DC: Author.

Helfgot, S. R. (2005). Core values and major issues in student affairs practice: What really matters. In S. R. Helfgot & M. M. Culp (Eds.), *New Directions for Community Colleges: No. 131. Community college student affairs: What really matters* (pp. 5–18). San Francisco, CA: Jossey-Bass.

Strayhorn, T. L. (2006). *Frameworks for assessing learning and development outcomes*. Washington DC: Council for the Advancement of Standards in Higher Education.

Tull, A., Hirt, J. B., & Saunders, S. (2009). *Becoming socialized in student affairs administration: A guide for new professionals and their supervisors*. Sterling, VA: Stylus.

ANNE M. HORNAK *is an associate professor of educational leadership at Central Michigan University.*

NEW DIRECTIONS FOR COMMUNITY COLLEGES • DOI: 10.1002/cc

6

The purpose of this chapter is to explore the integration of the ACPA/NASPA Professional Competency Areas for Student Affairs Practitioners (ACPA/NASPA, 2010) on community college campuses. The competencies provide specific skill sets for a broad range of student affairs practice areas that should be met by professionals throughout their careers. These competencies provide a tool to help assess and support staff development, and create clear performance expectations.

Professional Competencies for Student Affairs Practice

Patty Munsch, Lori Cortez

Professional competencies assist in staff assessment and development for student affairs professionals on community college campuses. Professional competencies serve as a guide to professional knowledge, expected skill sets, and areas of growth for student affairs professionals in the United States (ACPA/NASPA, 2010). The ACPA—College Student Educators International (ACPA) and NASPA—Student Affairs Administrators in Higher Education (NASPA) competencies intend to inform standards of excellence among student affairs professionals, regardless of their specific role and entry in student affairs. In 2010, a joint task force examined current literature to define the necessary skills, professional knowledge, and attitudes practitioners must develop and attain in the expansive field of student affairs. Developing from each competency are outcomes that practitioners are encouraged to incorporate in their practice. The focus of this chapter is to explore the competency areas through the lens of excellence in student affairs practice on community college campuses. As discussed in previous chapters the conceptual framework of excellence serves as the foundation of this chapter. Excellence in this context is the institutional or individual practices that engage students in learning. Furthermore, excellence will be used to describe actions that have proven through assessment to serve as best or promising practices.

In 1990, ACPA and NASPA along with the National Council on Student Development came together to establish the Student Affairs National

NEW DIRECTIONS FOR COMMUNITY COLLEGES, no. 166, Summer 2014 © 2014 Wiley Periodicals, Inc.
Published online in Wiley Online Library (wileyonlinelibrary.com) • DOI: 10.1002/cc.20101

Agenda in Community Colleges. The goal of the group was to create change on community college campuses that would support student success through student affairs. The team created a monograph and worksheets to be used by campus-level student affairs professionals (Floyd, 1991). In 1999, Marcus conducted research to determine the outcome of this endeavor. The research found that while the student body increased in ethnic diversity over the course of eight years, the demographics of the student affairs staff remained constant and there was no professional development to help staff understand the changing student demographic. Furthermore, the Student Affairs National Agenda in Community Colleges charged student affairs practitioners in community colleges to be more engaged in research and scholarship, but none of the participating colleges conducted any research during the eight-year review. Generally, the only individuals on campus to present during national and regional conferences were senior student affairs officers. Some colleges had student affairs practitioners who attended professional conferences; however, they did not engage in presentations or research. The research also found that community college student affairs staff often did not take advantage of professional development opportunities provided by their campus (Marcus, 1999).

This research speaks to the history and even the current state of student affairs at community colleges by providing a background of community college environments and current organizational trends. Practitioners in student affairs come from diverse educational backgrounds. For some community colleges, student affairs practitioners are required to hold a baccalaureate degree. Master's degrees required are often in counseling or mental-health-related areas, rather than within the field of higher education or student affairs. Community colleges do not recruit staff in the same format as many four-year institutions, keeping searches for student affairs staff local and without the support of major student affairs professional organizations. As a result, the student affairs staff often have not been exposed to major student affairs associations and are hesitant to get involved in or connected to their professional organizations, profiling the lack of cohesion among community college student affairs practices. The ACPA/NASPA professional competencies provide principles for community college student affairs practitioners and provide them with specific expectations with regard to standards of excellence.

Student affairs leaders can utilize the ACPA/NASPA competencies as a resource to support staff development. Through the use of the competencies, community college student affairs offices can come together to create a common understanding of practice in the field. The unified understanding will allow professionals the opportunity to evaluate their common practices then develop training to grow in competency areas to improve the quality of educational services on their campuses. The following are the competency areas listed in ACPA/NASPA (2010):

NEW DIRECTIONS FOR COMMUNITY COLLEGES • DOI: 10.1002/cc

- *Advising and helping.* It concentrates on advising referral, support, direction, and guidance.
- *Assessment, evaluation, and research.* It addresses the ability to design, implement, and evaluate qualitative and quantitative data.
- *Equity, diversity, and inclusion.* It focuses on creating learning environments that are inclusive of diverse people and views.
- *Ethical professional practice.* It works to integrate ethics into all areas of student affairs practice.
- *History, philosophy, and values.* It pertains to the connection between the premise of the profession and future growth.
- *Human and organizational resources.* It involves the management and empowerment of student affairs staff.
- *Law, policy, and governance.* It focuses on understanding shared governance and legal constructs.
- *Leadership.* It discusses the skills, knowledge, and attitude essential in a leader whom can anticipate, strategize, and implement change.
- *Personal foundations.* It addresses physical, emotional, and environmental introspection.
- *Student learning and development.* It involves the ability to apply theory to professional practice.

The ACPA/NASPA competencies are broken into 10 specific areas and within each area attributes are identified as basic, intermediate, and advanced. The focus of this section is to discuss each attribute, provide examples of student affairs practice that represents each area, and provide insights on how the attribute may be accomplished in different forms at community colleges. Advising and helping, as the first competency area serves to describe actions that counsel and "support through direction, feedback, critique, referral and guidance to individuals and groups" (ACPA/NASPA, 2010, p. 6). Generally, the attributes surrounding this competency include facilitation, managing conflict, collaboration, and crisis intervention. The actions connected with this ACPA/NASPA competency are based on working with students, peers, supervisors, and subordinates, and takes into account the multitude of functional areas that utilize such a skill set.

Within the dynamics of community colleges, advising and helping are often focused on enabling student learning in advising or counseling centers. A specific area identified in the competencies includes utilizing knowledge sources across campus. More than one half of community college students enroll in at least one developmental education course (Bailey, Jeong, & Cho, 2010). The student population is considered at-risk and as a result advising and help is a central concern for student retention. According to Fike and Fike (2008), "the strongest predictor of retention is passing a developmental reading course" (p. 80). Though curriculum is not generally considered an advisor's responsibility, advisors help the student by scheduling tutoring time between classes, thereby increasing their likelihood to pass developmental reading courses so strongly tied to their learning and academic retention. This holistic approach to student success strengthens the student, student affairs division, and the organization.

Assessment, evaluation, and research (AER), as a competency, focuses on the aptitude to conduct, manage, and utilize assessment, evaluation, and research in the practice of student affairs, and to engage the AER process as a function of the political climate. Through this ACPA/NASPA attribute, practitioners are expected to engage, design, evaluate, and critique forms of AER. The competency area links AER with learning outcomes and organizational goals and values with the expectation that through assessment, evaluation, and research student affairs will assess their learning outcomes. At community colleges in particular, learning outcomes are often directly linked to the organization's goals and values, thereby creating cohesion on campus that result in systemic, high-quality programs.

Equity, diversity, and inclusion explore the attributes of acceptance and celebration of differences by student affairs professionals, and understanding how to enrich environments with diverse views and people. Through this competency, professionals are expected to integrate culture, infuse social justice, and develop inclusive programs, services, and practices. Professionals need to demonstrate a commitment to advocacy, cultural knowledge, and continued self-reflection. The offices of student life on community college campuses often sponsor diversity and cultural awareness events. These events expose students, staff, and faculty who are typically from the surrounding area to cultures, religions, and ways of life that may not be prevalent in their local community but are prevalent in the globalized workforce, thereby preparing them for a life beyond academia.

The ACPA/NASPA competency of ethical professional practice guides, critiques, and integrates ethics into all aspects of self and professional practice. Actions connected with this competency include developing a set of personal ethical standards that adhere to professional ethical principles, recognizing and working to rectify incongruence in institutional practices, and articulating the role of ethics and integrity in discussions with students, peers, supervisors, and staff. Professionals should be able to identify and evaluate the ethical issues in the day-to-day operations of their job, develop ethical standards, and apply them to their relationships with colleagues and their student population.

The competency of history, philosophy, and values seeks to provide an in-depth understanding of the profession of student affairs. The expectation of this competency area includes a knowledge base of higher education history, foundational philosophies, institutional types, and various functional areas. By understanding the history, philosophy, and values, student affairs professionals build a stronger, more unified rationale for implementing programs and initiatives. Furthermore, according to ACPA/NASPA competencies, professionals should articulate their own professional values, engage in analysis of values and philosophy, and serve as teachers of our history.

Human and organizational resources refer to the ability to successfully manage staff, engage in bureaucratic processes effectively, and administer aspects of evolving college functions. The ACPA/NASPA competency incorporates aspects of facility management, crisis response, institutional liability, and resource allocation. This area also incorporates employment including job descriptions, staffing patterns, professional development, evaluations, and motivating others. Motivating personnel on community college campuses can often be a struggle as resources are typically more limited compared to universities. Whereas universities often have the capability of ensuring an employee's well-being and quality of employment through incentive, recognition, and recreational programs, community colleges often lack such human resources programs. Therefore, the burden of responsibility lies with departmental managers who must work to motivate, empower, and support employees who are declining in morale or becoming disengaged. These departmental motivations can come in the form of departmental recognitions and celebrations, social lunch gatherings, and peer-mentoring programs.

The competency of law, policy, and governance engages professionals in policy development through governance bodies within legal constructs. ACPA/NASPA attributes associated with this competency include an understanding of the system of higher education; the relationship between higher education and government; the role of law in higher education; the use and structure of higher education governance at the college, local, state, and national level; and implementing best practices with regard to access and affordability. Community college students often have less financial resources than their university counterparts, therefore requiring greater access to financial aid assistance and higher need for lower tuition costs (The Institute for College Access and Success, 2009). It is the responsibility of community college student affairs practitioners to ensure their students have access to financial aid programs and can afford to utilize college services, such as tutoring, fitness centers, computer labs, printers, and dining facilities, so vital to student engagement and retention (Kuh, 2003).

Leadership, as a competency, is described as the approach necessary to work collaboratively to imagine, map, and produce change. Through this lens, ACPA/NASPA competency attributes related to leadership include the ability to advocate for change, facilitate consensus, engage in governance, promote a shared vision, and create sustained systems for mentoring. An advanced student affairs practitioner provides leadership opportunities for employees by way of promoting them to lead initiatives, task force, committees, and advisory boards. The shared governance creates ownership among employees thereby allowing for shared vision and ease of change.

The personal foundations competency explores the holistic person within the professional and recognizes the importance of maintaining one's own emotional, physical, and social well-being. This competency involves remaining enthusiastic and inquisitive about your work. Characteristics related to this ACPA/NASPA professional competency involve identifying your own values and goals, utilizing reflection in your personal and professional life, improving your own wellness, and defining excellence for yourself. The practice of mindfulness is a quickly growing training resource in higher education whereby leaders pay close attention to their feelings, thoughts, and environment (Zakrzewski, 2013). In particular, mindfulness focuses on recognizing one's internal reaction to external environments that, as a result, intentionally elicits feelings of empathy and compassion, thereby creating plans, systems, and behaviors that ensure excellence in oneself and environment. In a recent study conducted by the University of Wisconsin's Center for Investigating Healthy Minds, educators who utilize mindfulness training reported improved behavior management skills and stronger emotional support for students (Zakrzewski, 2013).

Student learning and development engages professionals in knowledge acquisition centered on student development and learning theory. Through this competency professionals are expected to identify various types of student development theory, utilize theory to inform their practice, connect learning theories to learning outcomes, and assess such outcomes. This ACPA/NASPA competency attribute expects advanced professionals to analyze, critique, and contribute to the development of theories as well.

The ACPA/NASPA professional competencies for student affairs practitioners provide an opportunity to promote and unify student affairs professionals in excellence standards. The competencies not only identify points of practice but also include specific actions that individuals may engage in to significantly improve their professional knowledge, skills, and abilities. This, in turn, should increase the quality of student affairs and student learning on their campuses. Though not all competencies may apply to every student affairs practitioner evenly, the competencies encourage a shared individual excellence that facilitates student learning and development on campus.

References

ACPA—College Educators International & NASPA—Student Affairs Administrators in Higher Education (ACPA/NASPA). (2010). *Professional competency areas for student affairs practitioners.* Retrieved from http://www.naspa.org/images/uploads/main/Professional_Competencies.pdf

Bailey, T., Jeong, D. W., & Cho, S. W. (2010). Referral, enrollment, and completion in developmental education sequences in community colleges. *Economics of Education Review, 29*, 255–270.

Fike, D., & Fike, R. (2008). Predictors of first-year student retention in the community college. *Community College Review, 36*, 68–88.

Floyd, D. (1991). *Toward mastery leadership: Issues and challenges for the 1990s.* Iowa City, IA: American College Testing Program.

The Institute for College Access and Success. (2009). *Quick facts about financial aid and community colleges.* Retrieved from http://www.ticas.org/files/pub/cc_fact_sheet.pdf

Kuh, G. D. (2003). What we're learning about student engagement from NSSE: Benchmarks for effective educational practices. *Change, 35*(2), 24–32.

Marcus, L. R. (1999). Professional associations and student affairs policy. *Journal of College Student Development, 40,* 22–31.

Zakrzewski, V. (2013). *Can mindfulness make us better teachers?* The Greater Good Science Center, University of California, Berkeley. Retrieved from http://greatergood.berkeley.edu/article/item/can_mindfulness_make_us_better_teachers

PATTY MUNSCH *is a counselor and an associate professor of counseling at Suffolk County Community College.*

LORI CORTEZ *is a Title III Project Coordinator at Mid Michigan Community College.*

NEW DIRECTIONS FOR COMMUNITY COLLEGES • DOI: 10.1002/cc

The instruction and program quality at community colleges adheres to standards mandated through regional and national accreditation at institution and program levels. Community college personnel must understand their specific role in college and program accreditation and how accreditation is crucial for functions, such as accessing federal financial aid, guaranteeing credit hour transfers, and recognizing certification and licensure. The author presents an overview of the accreditation process and strategies for using the process to increase accountability.

Using Professional Standards for Higher Education to Improve Student Affairs

Renay M. Scott

Student affairs professionals need to understand the process of accreditation and its role in increasing accountability and effectively serving students. Community colleges enroll nearly 50% of all students in the United States. President Barack Obama brought even more attention to the community college movement by emphasizing that in the future more jobs will require at least an associate degree. As more than six million students enter community colleges each fall seeking affordable tuition, flexible programs, and convenient locations, student affairs programs have expanded to support those students and are beginning to include more programs typically found at the four-year college and university, such as residential programs, honors programs, and study-abroad programs. These have been added to the more traditional community college programs, such as TRIO programs, orientation, advising, internships, and disability resources.

As student affairs personnel at community colleges become more actively involved with more and more programs to support student learning, understanding standards and the assessment of those programs based upon those standards will be an ever-increasing component of the job and will be necessary to answer questions of quality and compatibility when recruiting or retaining students. Additionally, understanding accreditation will assist student affairs personnel in helping the college comply with institutional

NEW DIRECTIONS FOR COMMUNITY COLLEGES, no. 166, Summer 2014 © 2014 Wiley Periodicals, Inc.
Published online in Wiley Online Library (wileyonlinelibrary.com) • DOI: 10.1002/cc.20102

accreditation requirements and federal financial aid requirements, and be more knowledgeable when participating in accreditation activities. Specifically, student affairs personnel need a deep understanding of the CAS Professional Standards for Higher Education to ensure that student affairs programs are implemented based upon best practice to ensure the institution meets its goals for student persistence, retention, and completion.

Accreditation has been a part of higher education culture for over one hundred years and is a means of distinguishing postsecondary study from secondary education (American Council of Education, 2012). Accreditation is considered a voluntary, peer-review process whereby community colleges adhere to a set of standards. Accreditation can be achieved at the institutional level and at the program level. In the United States, regional and national accreditation commissions ensure that community colleges meet standards of quality through regular and cyclical monitoring. Each of the regional and national accreditation commissions is accountable to the Department of Education.

Today, institution-wide accreditation is required for institutions to be able to award federal financial aid to students. Program-level accreditation is often necessary for community colleges for several reasons. First, it is necessary when community colleges wish to have their degree or credit hours transferred to a four-year college or university and is often necessary for programs at a community college to award industry recognized certification or licensure. Industry certification or licensure is often linked to a required state or national test that graduates from an accredited program must take in order to be awarded the appropriate credential. In addition to program-level accreditation, there are a number of specialty accreditations that add value. For example, honors programs, digital learning programs, and leadership programs have opportunities to be accredited. Each level of accreditation follows a similar process of self review and peer review based upon established criteria. Within the student affairs division of the college, the Council for the Advancement of Standards in Higher Education (CAS) includes general standards for over 43 student affairs areas.

Institutional Accreditation and Student Affairs

Community colleges in the United States seek accreditation through a regional accrediting organization. The Council for Higher Education Accreditation identifies six regional accreditation organizations. While institutional and program accreditation is often considered an activity for the academic division within the community college, the standards of quality do not just focus on the teaching and learning that takes place in the classroom. Accreditation standards at both the institutional and program level also address practices in business affairs, academic support areas, and student affairs. For example, regional accreditation bodies are becoming concerned with processes and practices within the student affairs division. For example,

NEW DIRECTIONS FOR COMMUNITY COLLEGES • DOI: 10.1002/cc

the Higher Learning Commission of the North Central States accreditation standard 3.D. focuses on student services. Standard 3.D. states, "The institution provides support for student learning and effective teaching." Two of the specific criteria under standard 3.D. specifically related to student services personnel are:

- 3.D.1. The institution provides student support services suited to the needs of its student populations.
- 3.D.3. The institution provides academic advising suited to its programs and the needs of its students. (HLC, 2012, "Criteria for Accreditation," Section 3.D.)

Institutional accrediting commissions do not only include standards that address services provided directly to students but they also include standards to ensure the quality of the administrative processes within the student affairs division. For example, the Southern Association of Colleges and Schools' standard 3.9 specifically defines best practices within the student affairs division related to student conduct, student records, and the credential of employees within the student affairs division. The standards include the following:

- 3.9.1. The institution publishes a clear and appropriate statement of student rights and responsibilities and disseminates the states to the campus community. (Student rights)
- 3.9.2. The institution protects the security, confidentiality, and integrity of student records and maintains security measures to protect and back up data. (Student records)
- 3.9.3. The institution provides a sufficient number of qualified staff—with appropriate education or experience in the student affairs areas—to accomplish the mission of the institution. (Qualified staff) (Southern Association of Colleges and Schools Commission on Colleges [SACSCOC], 2011, p. 31)

Consequently, student affairs personnel are becoming more and more involved with institutional and program accreditations.

Program or Specialty Accreditation

Program-level accreditation serves the same function as institutional, regional accreditation, to ensure quality. The main difference is that program accreditation is more narrowly focused than institutional accreditation in that the focus is on the specific professional program. Program-level accreditation involves the review of the program based upon specific standards for the profession. Program accreditation follows a similar process as institutional accreditation that includes the submission of a self-study, peer review, and further review by a board of governance that makes the final decision to grant initial accreditation or reauthorize existing accreditation. A key feature of program accreditation is the peer review of the program. Within this step, the site visitation team is comprised of individuals who are professionals within the field of study. Institutional accreditation includes peer review as well, but often peer reviewers are from various divisions commonly found at an institution, such as presidents, provosts, business affairs personnel, and student affairs personnel.

For some professional programs, specialty accreditation is optional. However, for some professional programs, specialty accreditation is a required component for the program in order to have graduates in the program sit for the licensure exam or be granted credentials to enter the profession. Often these requirements vary by state rather than program. Student affairs professionals need to be aware of these requirements and differences so when they are recruiting students they can represent these requirements appropriately. Further, student affairs personnel may be involved in developing communication strategies to current and potential students about professional programs. Representing accreditation and credential requirements within communication plans or recruitment plans is vital to ensuring accurate communication to students and stakeholders.

Many institutional and program accreditation organizations require communication about the status of accreditation to the public. Many accreditation organizations require that an institution report to students when a program or institution remains on accreditation but is accredited with conditions. Once a program or institution achieves accreditation a regular review process follows a predetermined cycle. Accreditation decisions generally include several distinctions. An institution or program can receive full reauthorization without conditions, or it may receive reauthorization with conditions. Often when an institution or program is reauthorized with conditions, an annual follow up report or in severe cases a follow up visit may be required. Institutions and programs can be placed on probation if the reauthorization process uncovers significant, unaddressed issues that need attention. In each of these reauthorization classifications, the institution may look to student affairs personnel to ensure that the appropriate institutional or program status is included on promotion or communication materials to students specific to the program or institution. It is important for student affairs personnel to understand the requirements of institutional and program accreditation to communicate accurately to students on promotional materials.

Council for the Advancement of Standards in Higher Education

At times, the academic division of the college looks suspiciously at the student affairs division because of the discussions about affective components of the student experience. Periodically, the academic division defines learning narrowly, being comprised of the activities that take place solely within the classroom. However, learning within the classroom is impacted by the events within a student's life both on campus and off campus. The division of student affairs is uniquely designed to support learning within the classroom. Student affairs professionals, leading programs of excellence, have developed professional standards as a means of professionalizing the activities of the student affairs division.

The Council for the Advancement of Standards in Higher Education (CAS) is the student affairs equivalent to program accreditation for the academic division. CAS was founded in 1979 and is the leading institution for promoting standards for student affairs, student services, and student development programs. CAS is not accreditation, per se, but is an organization that provides research based standards by which an institution can assess the quality of their individual student affairs programs.

The Council for the Advancement of Standards in Higher Education has developed a set of general standards and self-assessment tools for accountability and evaluation in over 43 program areas under the purview of student affairs personnel (CAS, 2012). These standards include a rating scale to make institutional review of the service areas easy and informative. CAS standards are available for over 43 student affairs programs ranging from A to Z including such traditional community college programs as:

- Academic advising
- Adult learner programs and services
- Career services
- College honor societies
- Disability resources and services
- International student programs and services
- Internship programs
- Multicultural student programs and services
- Orientation programs
- Registrar programs and services
- Service-learning programs
- Student conduct programs
- TRIO and other educational opportunity programs
- Veterans and military programs and services
- Women student programs and services

The CAS standards provide an opportunity for student affairs personnel to engage in the same self-study process that institutional or program accreditation offers, but targeted in one or more of the traditional student affairs programs. An institutionally appointed self-assessment team can use the CAS standards to engage in a self-study. The self-study can identify and summarize institutional practices, identify discrepancies between institutional practices and the standards, and develop a plan of action to address the discrepancies. Another use of the CAS standards is for institutional planning of a new program. Recently, one community college in Ohio utilized the CAS standards to present a proposal to the executive leadership team to expand the institution's international programs and study abroad experiences. The value of utilizing CAS standards for design and evaluation of student affairs programs is that the standards place an emphasis on student learning and student development within the student support areas.

Recently, one Midwestern community college vice president of student affairs was approached by a small group of students requesting a meeting. The nature of the meeting was to request a prayer room on campus to accommodate their need for a private place for religious observances. The vice president of student affairs assembled a small team of student affairs employees to examine the CAS standards related to Campus Religious and Spiritual Programs and to survey other community colleges in the region. The college wished to not only accommodate those students who met with the vice president of student affairs but also others who may not have realized how to go about approaching the college pertaining to their spiritual needs.

An Eastern community college located in a suburban area of a large city employed a mix security and police force on the campus. The campus also utilized a Behavioral Consultation Team to review student conduct referrals on campus and to monitor individual students' behavior in a variety of settings on campus as needed. The Behavioral Consultation Team was also responsible for developing, monitoring, and revising the campus safety plan. As the team began to discuss the current campus safety plan and examine student conduct data from the previous three years, the team decided to utilize the CAS standards on Campus Police and Security Programs to conduct a self-assessment. After completing the self-assessment, the team concluded that changes needed to be made to the campus' safety division. The Behavioral Consultation Team made a recommendation to the college president and trustees to move the division to a campus police force. The recommendation included the CAS self-assessment, a budget analysis, a coverage analysis, and a summary of best practices for other institutions of similar size that had transitioned from a mixed security and police force to a complete police force.

The Council for the Advancement of Standards in Higher Education has also developed a set of characteristics for individuals who practice in student affairs. These characteristics attempt to establish the competencies necessary for student affairs and other professionals who plan, implement, and offer programs in student affairs. The standards address the following areas:

- Administration and management
- Multicultural awareness, knowledge, and skills
- Helping and advising
- Assessment and research

- Teaching and training
- Ethics and professional standards
- Translation and use of theory to guide practice

Such standards can serve as a set of criteria for institutions to develop job descriptions and conduct employment searches that assists the institution in hiring individuals who can ensure that student affairs programs are designed, administered, and offered keeping the best practices at the forefront.

Summary

Increasingly, the federal government and general public are calling for greater accountability in higher education. The growing desire for accountability in higher education has manifested itself in the evolution of the national completion agenda. As the completion agenda begins to enter educational policy at the state level, community colleges will need to examine their academic, business, and student affairs practices to ensure that they are designed to support student persistence, retention, and completion. Student affairs divisions often include many of the programs that help students establish a relationship with the college, further increasing their chances of persistence and retention. As academic divisions respond to institutional and program accreditation standards which are beginning to include standards applicable to student affairs personnel, the Council of the Advancement of Standards in Higher Education has developed a robust set of standards for over 43 student affairs personnel. These standards serve as the basis for self-assessment, leading to program improvement. Further, these standards can serve as the basis for initial program design within the student affairs division of the college. Student affairs personnel need to become more involved with institutional accreditation and also need to utilize the CAS standards at the program level to ensure support for institutional measures of student persistence, retention, and completion.

References

American Council of Education. (2012). *Assuring academic quality in the 21st century: Self-regulation in a new era*. Washington DC: Author.

Council for the Advancement of Standards in Higher Education (CAS). (2012). *CAS professional standards for higher education* (8th ed.). Washington, DC: Author.

Higher Learning Commission (HLC). (2012). *The criteria for accreditation and core components*. Retrieved from http://www.ncahlc.org/Criteria-Eligibility -and-Candidacy/criteria-and-core-components.html

Southern Association of Colleges and Schools Commission on Colleges (SACSCOC). (2011). *Principles of accreditation: Foundation for quality enhancement* (5th ed.). Retrieved from http://www.sacscoc.org/pdf/2012PrinciplesOfAcreditation.pdf

RENAY M. SCOTT *is the president of Dona Ana Community College.*

8

In this chapter, the author draws on this volume's chapters to identify prominent issues and challenges facing student affairs professionals. Suggestions for practice are provided that support the work of professionals to create quality educational environments.

Creating and Implementing Practices That Promote and Support Quality Student Affairs Professionals

Steve Tyrell

The role of the student affairs professional at community colleges continues to evolve and expand as the student experience is understood with greater complexity in the field of student affairs and as community colleges have broadened their role in how they engage students in and outside of the classroom. The prior chapters raise a series of key considerations for the student affairs professional at community colleges, and professionals must weigh their implications if colleges are to successfully organize the student affairs organization within the opportunities and constraints emerging in the near future. Student completion rates, default rates, debates on placement in the workforce that closes the skills gap (whether advanced manufacturing or otherwise) are examples of external pressures community colleges must consider in how best to organize a credible student affairs organization. There are emerging trends in the student affairs profession that also must be customized to fit the mold of the community college experience.

This chapter will contextualize those considerations in a manner that honors the past traditions of the community college experience while also reshaping the student affairs organization to address the needs of the future of this higher education sector.

The Credentialed Professional

Our most valuable asset in our higher education organization is the human resource. In Chapter 2, Lunceford forwarded the assertion that many see the acquisition of a master's degree requisite for admission into the

NEW DIRECTIONS FOR COMMUNITY COLLEGES, no. 166, Summer 2014 © 2014 Wiley Periodicals, Inc.
Published online in Wiley Online Library (wileyonlinelibrary.com) • DOI: 10.1002/cc.20103

profession. She also posits that not any master's degree is sufficient, and that one in a student-development-related degree is required for the practitioner. In Chapter 6, Munsch and Cortez also explore the implications of a baccalaureate prepared professional and reengage the role of graduate preparation in defining the credentialed professional. The debate surrounding the credentialed professional has heated up in the profession in recent years and this debate has also arrived at the doorstep of the community college. The profession has discussed certification for years (Arminio et al., 2006; Janosik & Carpenter, 2005); it is surely still controversial to the profession, and for many mid-level managers and SSAOs, certification may even appear threatening to their current level of professional credentials. Perhaps this is why the student affairs profession has not come to closure on certification for student affairs professionals. The consideration of credentialed student affairs professionals by professional organizations is a key component of an evolved student affairs organization. ACPA (Love et al., 2007) and NASPA/ACPA (Bresciani et al., 2010) both have identified the 10 core competency categories for the profession. These competencies were also surveyed by Tyrell et al. (2005). Seven of the 10 competency categories were earlier surveyed by Walter, Fey, Cortese, and Borg (1991). These seven core professional competencies: leadership, fiscal management, professional development, personnel management, student contact, communication, and research and evaluation have remained consistent for two decades, and in the last five years we have seen a few additional categories identified (technology, culture, diversity/pluralism and inclusion, professional self). They all represent important areas of professional development for the profession. Today, these 10 categories are considered core to the credential professional. There are various forms of discussions that give context to being "credentialed"; some being formalized, some being traditional, and other less so but just as valued.

The traditional sense of being credentialed is situated around the acquisition of an advanced degree. The movement toward entry-level professionals with master's degrees in higher education or student development has been upon the profession for more than a decade, yet it is not evident that this traditional form of credential has caught up to the community college sector. Beyond the banter that exists regarding credential creep, the greater question at hand is the assessed value of the advanced degree for the community college entry-level professional. The emergence of the student development models over the course of the last 40 years asserts that our students are comprised of a wide diversity of maturation issues and human needs. The complexity of the human condition that connects to the diversity of students represented on our campuses promotes the importance of professionals acquiring an advanced degree that is focused on serving our community college students.

It would seem that 40 years of research on the matter of student maturation and the human needs related to the student experience serves as a guide for how the student affairs professional approaches their work today. There is some debate in the profession how these theories and models are applied in the everyday work of the professional. However, although these theories and models never intended to exclude the student affairs professional's work in the community college sector, the student development framework embedded in the work of the practitioner appears to be marginalized or altogether absent here. We can only posit why this has occurred. For some, there may be the assertion that the matter of student maturation and growth is less prevalent on community colleges with the absence of residence halls. Nevertheless, one could argue that the challenges these students face in their lives may not have played out in a residential setting, but they are certainly evident in the classroom, club activities, team sports, student competitions, and student government in the community college setting. Furthermore, with the burgeoning number of residence halls on community colleges today, many community colleges offer many of the same services and student life programs that have been central to the residential experience found at baccalaureate colleges for decades. Another reason might be that there seems to be fewer student affairs professionals in the community college sector who have completed graduate work embedded with student development formal training than their peers in the four-year sector. If this is true, but the student maturation and growth transitions are similar across all higher education sectors, the community college professional should (re)consider how they could best obtain the training necessary to effectively apply these student development models within the learning environments where these students learn and live. We thus believe there are a number of reasons why the community college professional should consider being competent in applying student development theories and models with community college students.

The current debate within professional associations in student affairs echoes the same emphasis of the importance of professionals understanding the development and human needs of our student populations, which can only be acquired through the acquisition of an advance degree—or is that truly the case? ACPA's credentialing implementation team is tackling this very question as it believes that there are professionals who can demonstrate the knowledge competencies and skills sets necessary to effectively interact with, and support and challenge our students, and do so in absence of an advance degree. How is this possible? There is a belief that professionals can acquire skills sets through seeking out professional development opportunities (e.g., read a text on Student Development Theory to Practice, study articles, take a class on the subject matter, create a campus-base student development theory to practice seminar for professionals). Many of us in the profession struggle with the answer surrounding the debate of the graduate degree requirement. Some of us are convinced that the acquisition of a graduate degree in student-development-related programs is a *necessary condition* for a basic level of preparation for a professional working with students but it is not a *sufficient condition* for demonstration of effectively working with individuals in a robust learning environment. The key though is the professional must seek the information that resides in the degree credential and necessary information that resides elsewhere, and this acquisition of knowledge competencies is ongoing throughout one's career if they are to be successful. The graduate degree is a credential for entering the profession but it cannot be the end-all for the professional. New models emerge each year as shifts occur in the student populations studied. Learning environments also continue to shift and impact on the shape of the experience student have in their journey of growth and maturation, skill acquisition, and their understanding of an increasingly more complex and smaller world. Professionals will be successful in serving their students' learning and their campuses if they commit to a lifetime of professional development.

Invest and Diversify in Your Professional Development

A strong professional development plan is essential for any student affairs professional. For those who reside in the community college sector, the plan would include many topics that one would find elsewhere in the profession (such as leadership development, fiscal management, personnel management, effective advising, use of technology in student affairs applications, conflict resolution, and effective communication; Love et al., 2007; Tyrell & Farmer, 2006). But the community college professional also has to consider developing skills and knowledge competencies associated with developing community/external relations, child care services, student retention strategies in and outside of the classroom, and workforce training (beyond the scope of career development and career advising) if they are to round out their professional portfolio.

It is also important to recognize the implications of our hallmarks of the student affairs profession, our national conventions and academic journals, each of which professes access for the professional to professional development. Nevertheless, many of the seven skill sets and knowledge competencies considered core to the profession in 1989 and still today are not easily accessible to professionals through their participation in these hallmarks of the profession. Tyrell and Fey (in press) sampled the broad array of journal articles and professional development sessions offered at conventions over the course of the last decade, and many of the seven professional competencies espoused by ACPA and NASPA are absent. Again, it is important to state here that these current convention programs and scholarly works are important in regard to understanding the complexity inherent in the human condition and the environments with which we interface with students.

But our interest and allocation of convention and journal space to the complexity of the human condition of our campuses has left little room for professional development in many of the other core competency areas;

in most cases other professional competencies (i.e., leadership, personnel management, communication, and fiscal management) are almost nonexistent in these hallmarks of the profession. So, as a professional interested in advancing their core professional competencies, one must look elsewhere if one is to gather the full gamut of competencies necessary for today. More so, we believe there is also merit if these hallmarks of the profession took an additional step forward and further contextualized how we prepare student affairs professionals in the community college sector to be effective in the application of these professional competencies. For instance, we believe the introductory level of fiscal management would be very similar for professionals across higher education sectors. For the intermediate level, we believe the nature of higher education funding diverges between the community college sector and other public college sectors, whereas here a convention session or a journal article might illuminate those differences and how they affect the work of the professional and others. This type of closer inspection regarding where similarities and differences occur for student affairs professionals among the higher education sectors is really important for the hallmarks of the profession if they are interested in continuing to expand their commitment to community college professionals.

Thus, there are other less traditional avenues for developing the credentialed professional that may be formal (e.g., a regional seminar) or informal (e.g., a coach who assists the professional on acquiring or strengthening a skill or knowledge competency). In some instances, the best practices in training student affairs professionals in fiscal management, personnel management, conflict resolution, and effective advising may in fact be found outside of our hallmarks of the profession and even outside of our profession. There are other higher education associations that provide training in the seven core competencies noted earlier. NACUBO provides excellent training in fiscal management. ACUHO provides credentialing support in the areas of supervision and other critical elements of personnel and facilities management programs. Best practices in training on leadership and professional communications are often found outside of student affairs professional associations and higher education, and are often situated in the American corporate sector or the European public sector. Collaboration strategies and constructing effective partnerships (the latter an essential element in the operation of a community college) are offered through workforce development boards in many of our communities. You have to shop around if you wish to develop the core competencies for a community college professional. In the end, the credentialed professional is not truly measured by what they know or what they attended for professional development opportunities. They are measured by their *ability to effectively apply* their knowledge competencies and skills sets (however acquired) in their interactions with their students, other campus constituents, and external entities with close relationships established with the community college. The conversation on credentialing is a volatile one in the profession at this time;

nevertheless, the merit of identifying core competencies and knowledge bases necessary for student affairs professionals is paramount in designing a right-sized, right-themed organization for community colleges. So, where does this leave us for the credentialed professional at the community college? Let's use the application of a credential in how we might approach recruiting student affairs staff at a community college. We would design entry-level and mid-level managerial positions around knowledge competencies and skills sets (see Love et al., 2007) versus job descriptions that focus solely on job functions. We would approach the candidate interview differently as credentialed employers looking for competent and credentialed employees. For example, candidates should be able to demonstrate application of knowledge competencies and skills sets required for the position in job interviews. We could provide a candidate with a scenario regarding two or three students in conflict, who have varying and diverse backgrounds, and ask the candidate, "What student development theories are at play here and what do those theories inform you about what might be the most effective approach you would use as a professional to help these students resolve the matter between them?" After all, a student affairs professional must be able to demonstrate how they manage "supporting and challenging" students as the professional navigates a myriad of human dynamics embedded in our students' histories. "Winging it" with the student or "doing what I did when I was a student" or "treating everyone the same way" are axioms for disaster for any community college professional who wishes to invest in their professional development and work in our vibrant and exciting communities of human diversity. Are you prepared to answer this question in an interview; more importantly, are you prepared to serve your students with this level of complexity in your work? You must acquire those behaviors and attitudes of the profession requisite for success and to be effective as a student affairs professional today.

The A Word: *Assessment*

A second consideration—one that serves many masters, including accreditation, strategic planning, financial forecasting, and student completion—is the matter of assessment. Some student affairs professionals might even lament that these noted items are not in the purview of their everyday work in community colleges. At a recent seminar, a colleague lamented that student affairs professionals were told by academic affairs leadership that completion was not a concern of theirs. We know, however, that student completion (the acquisition of an academic credential) is a reflection of student persistence and student engagement. We also know that students persist and are engaged in many different ways in the community college in and outside of the classroom, and in many instances, the lines are blurred nicely between these two worlds. Student retention, persistence, and completion are everyone's responsibility.

Whether it is assessment tied to student completion, strategic planning, accreditation (under the rubric of measuring institutional effectiveness), or financial forecasting, the community college professional has to collect *meaningful* data to ensure their effectiveness. In Chapter 1, Knight reminds us that professionals who constantly build best practices by looking to measure their efforts are achieving the results they desire. In Chapter 5, Hornak discusses the importance of the role the CAS standards can have in informing us of the effectiveness of our work and how it is a comprehensive tool for assessing many dimensions of our work, our results, and how we structure the work setting to promote and assess student learning. In Chapter 7, Scott picks up the discussion of student learning and assessment and contextualizes it in the role accreditation plays for the student affairs professional. Assessment, whether focused in student learning outcomes or program outcomes beyond the scope of learning, has become both form and function for the student affairs professional today.

It is also important that we discern that the discussion on assessment in higher education today has taken a huge leap forward from what it might have been two decades ago. Today, meaningful assessment is not to be confused with mandated reporting (albeit in some cases, they may be one in the same). Meaningful assessment data are data you will use to make decisions regarding the effectiveness of your current program offerings and student services and what data you need to determine how you can best improve your programs. Stated differently, good assessment is not about collecting data and storing it on a shelf to collect dust, it is largely knowing what data you need to insure you are reaching for and eventually achieving those key performance indicators that denote a quality student affairs program and/or experience for your students.

More specifically, the matter of community college student affairs professionals developing the skill sets and knowledge competencies to effectively collect, analyze, and report out data-driven decisions tied to outcomes-based results is required henceforth. The politicized discussion at the federal and state level regarding student completion may be a blessing or a curse for community colleges when all is said and done. But these issues are here to stay, and it will require the community college professional to develop strong assessment and intervention programs for boosting student retention that eventually leads to completion.

The practice of effective assessment is part art and part science. There is a science to using credible, reliable, and valid approaches to making claims regarding how the data collected and analyzed inform you whether you have had an impact on retention and/or completion. There is an art to creating clearly defined outcomes you wish to achieve. You can overcomplicate or underwhelm your set desired outcome and either never complete the assessment activity or achieve results that are meaningless. So, to do it well, become proficient at both the art form and the science of assessment. The SMART approach to creation of assessment outcomes is to define outcomes objectives that are Specific in describing what you intend to assess; to establish concrete criteria for Measuring progress toward the objective; to assert something will be gained or improved versus measuring what you simply do (Aggressive but Attainable); and to define objectives that are Results-oriented in that the objective is central to the organization and its success, and are Time-bound in that the assessment activity occurs in a specific (and often narrow) period of time.

There are many ways to learn assessment techniques and what applications and methods of analysis will yield the most meaningful results. One good rule of thumb regarding developing proficiency is to dive into the work quickly and often so that you can build your skill. Another good rule of thumb in assessment is to study what your institution needs to know versus what you are interested in knowing. Sometimes the stars do align and they are one and the same. But I have seen one too many assessment reports that assessed what one well-meaning professional was interested in, but it did not have relevancy to the institutional strategic plan's initiative, accreditation benchmarks, or student retention and completion. In regard to retention and completion, good assessment programs are not those that might have an impact on retention or might have a correlation to completion. Good assessment programs today demonstrate where our strengths and gaps are in delivering programs and services that clearly impact completion and retention.

There are good completion indices to focus our future assessment efforts and some are more relevant than others depending on the type of academic culture that exists at your campus and the specific needs of the students targeted in the completion effort. Completion indices are defined as predictors of student likelihood to either persist or fail to complete. Completion indices can be student-bound or institutional-related. Predemographic indicators (e.g., high school GPA) are good predictors of student completion, but often are not useful in implementation of an intervention strategy to support those students who are lower on predemographic scales than their peers. Midterm grades are necessary data points for retention analysis but acted upon as impetuses for follow-up intervention are often too late to have a serious impact.

Good completion indices that have emerged as effective for predicting student completion are tied to a variety of student skills and attitudinal attributes. They include *student performance variables*, such as (a) student successful completion of a math class in senior year of high school; (b) the minimal number of required remedial courses sequenced prior to a math/composition course that counts toward the degree; (c) attendance during the first three classes of the term; (d) completion of homework assignments; (e) student level of engagement in the classroom; (f) limited number of times a student repeats a course; (g) (surprisingly) student's ability to articulate name of instructor; and (h) student competency with application of various academic support skills (i.e., note-taking, test preparation, time management program, and established study regimen). They also include *student attitudinal variables*, such as (a) the ability for students early on in a course to attach relevancy between course work and their life/career experiences; (b) student attitude toward engagement in institutional programs and activities outside of the classroom; (c) ability for students to articulate academic/career goals early on in college experience; (d) the student's ability to establish targets for academic performance milestones earlier on in college experience; and (e) student's description of relationship with their campus employer (supervisor or supervisor/mentor). Student affairs professionals in the community college sector recognize the importance of determining how these completion indices drive their interactions with students and how they design programs that promote and support successful student completion. Very often, many of these completion indices are presented to students through advising efforts and through presentation of materials in first year (and highest success in first term) experience courses.

Institutional completion indices are those that are described as institutional practices that signal red flag possibilities that a student may be hitting a barrier toward successful completion. Examples include (a) student's failure to register due to institutional holds; (b) failure to apply for a degree; (c) student's rating of quality of advisor/faculty plan for student to follow upon return from academic dismissal; (d) institutional policy on course repeats; (e) policy on late registrations; (f) requirement to meet with advisor as part of course registration; (g) policy on referral (mandated or voluntary); and (h) correlating tutoring sessions (frequency and quality of) with students at-risk's GPAs. Whether student-based or institutional-related, these completion indices as identified sites of analysis can lead to outcomes assessment work related to student satisfaction, student persistence and retention, and eventually student completions that are specific objectives that are measurable, aggressive but attainable, results-oriented, and time-bound once a specific objective is set. The SMART approach to outcomes assessment is also analogous to any strategic plan focused on achieving results that drive institutional effectiveness. The community college student affairs professional is engaged in many of the completion indices described here and can partner with others to engage in meaningful assessment activities.

Politicizing the Student Completion Agenda?

The list of completion indices provided here are hardly comprehensive. Yet they represent the complexity and variables that affects student completion. The student affairs professional at community colleges has to develop those skills to effectively assess student completion and to administer programs and services that support students to move beyond those challenges and barriers that impede student completion. The focus on student completion has not been delimited to the student affairs professionals, as it is also a commitment long held by others in academe and collectively it epitomizes the long commitment and large amount of resources community colleges have dedicated to student completion. Achieving success with student completion is challenging because so many variables that affect student completion are out of the control of the institution. But student affairs professionals and their academic colleagues at community colleges continue to develop incredible intervention programs to increase success with student completion. Unfortunately, the recent politicizing of student completion by external entities is having a dangerous effect on redirecting our core commitment to student learning and student success.

Politicians at the federal level and in some states across the country have looked at low completion rates at community colleges (and in comparison to their baccalaureate counterparts) and have decided that performance-based funding for institutions of higher education should be primarily based on student completion. This is a mistake for many reasons, but one that is important to mention here is that the formula for calculating student completion is flawed and primarily disadvantages the community college sector. The mistake is that student completion and funding is currently based on *where* the student finally completes the degree (per the federal use of IPEDS) and does not account for those other institutions who have contributed to where student completed academic work before arriving at the institution where the degree was awarded. A new and more robust formula for crediting course completion is required if performance-based funding is to be strongly tethered to student completion. We also know that many students attend community colleges with no intention of completing a degree there. Some have suggested that funding agencies should only penalize funding to college for those students who self-identify they were seeking a degree and failed to complete. Neither case for a fairer application of performance-based funding has been addressed by funding entities. If you are still questioning the potential ill effect that performance-based funding tethered to student completion can have on colleges, simply look at the ill effect federal financial aid progress has had on student learning and, in some instances, student completion. How does a student today explore career options in college without risk of loss of financial aid if the consequence of that exploration could be loss of aid and dropping out of college? These formulaic approaches to student completion, albeit well-intentioned at its inception years ago to create a level playing field in funding student academic progress, has only made completion less accessible and more difficult for students who face other obstacles in life. We are fearful that these conditional purse strings only result in a reduction of funding to those community colleges and could potentially increase completion but have a dangerous ripple effect on access to students who are less prepared. Open access to community colleges has been one of the bastions of promoting the American dream. Open access will be a commitment community colleges can ill afford to maintain if performance-based funding brings its full weight to bear on community colleges. Student affairs professionals will need to take a center stage role in asserting to our many publics the ramifications of any current or new effort that may unintentionally limit access to higher education to those for whom community college is their only hope. We need to make sure our higher education leaders, our federal and state legislators, our students, parents, and county sponsors are fully informed of the impact of performance-based funding and that if it is legislated, it is done so in a manner that we don't allow well-intentioned accountability marginalize access to higher education and reduce hope to only a distant dream.

In Chapter 3, the discussion on the exercise of unobtrusive control mechanisms for the mid-level manager speaks to the politicizing of work in everyday interactions with supervisors, peers, and employees. These forms of unobtrusive control are also descriptions of actions layered on everyday interactions with other publics. They are possible templates for how student affairs professionals can choose to engage respective politicos, students, parents, and others in new forms of everyday discourse with these stakeholders. Although student affairs professionals do not always see themselves as having the means to influence and broaden the current discussion with the larger powers that be, they must play a role in making the current discussion more transparent. Our students and institutions have much to lose if we remain silent much longer. The full impact and potential outcomes that performance-based funding may have on the student completion discussion is not clear. We may lose more than student access in the long run. Student affairs professionals are stakeholders in this conversation. They can effectively lead the discussion with regional, state, and federal stakeholders who are committed to student completion but who may not recognize the unintended outcomes and consequences if this funding movement takes full hold of higher education.

Student Learning Outcomes Assessment

Performance-based funding is not only tied to the conversation of student completion, it is also tied to other institutional outcomes. In some states, student learning outcomes assessment is also linked to performance-based funding. In addition, accreditation bodies, state legislatures, parents, and other stakeholders also have recently called upon colleges to demonstrate where and to what degree student learning occurs outside of the classroom. The case has also been made for student affairs professionals to engage in *student learning outcomes assessment* efforts for some time now (Hanson, 1988). Hanson wrote two decades ago that the research agenda for student affairs will be dictated by the purposes behind the assessment of students. He emphasized the importance of accountability to the college as a primary purpose for conducting assessment and that student learning and student development must be assessed if we are to improve ourselves as educators (Hanson, 1988, pp. 54–57). Hanson identified one of the important, if not essential, parts of our work as a student affairs professional is that our assessment efforts should also be tied to student learning. In recent years, the federal government has pushed for greater accountability (Spellings Commission, 2006). The increased emphasis on accountability measures for higher education should include all campus professionals, including student affairs. To remain a vital and viable part of the higher education community in the future, the community college student affairs professional must embrace student learning outcomes assessment.

If the old adage holds true that 80% of what a student learns in college, they learn outside of the classroom, what are they learning and where are they learning it? The latter point could simply be anywhere, but from an outcomes assessment standpoint, what are students learning as they interact with community college professionals in student activities, student leadership programs, residence life, new student orientation, advising and tutoring, judicial affairs, mediation, health services, counseling services, multicultural affairs, civic engagement and service learning, study abroad programs, financial aid, athletics and recreation, and the list goes on ... for possible learning sites of interaction and engagement? Students report that they learn from student affairs professionals through various learning delivery systems: one-on-one interactions, group settings, and passive and active programming. Student affairs provide programs and services that represent a cross section of critical knowledge competencies and skill sets we often espouse as institutional values (such as leadership, effective communication, ability to successfully interact and navigate in a multicultural global society, and serve as a team player). These knowledge competencies listed can also be further divided into specific learning outcomes, such as conflict resolution, financial literacy, ethical decision making, collaboration, conflict resolution, coping with stress, health management, problem solving, academic skills development, organizational skill building, fiscal management, delegating skills, motivating others, self-esteem and self-worth management, cognitive complexity, and postformal reasoning.

It is clear that student learning is central to the work of student affairs professionals. And thus student learning outcomes assessment is as much a part of the professional's responsibility to measure student learning as that of the faculty member in the classroom. The SMART approach to developing student learning outcomes assessment is largely similar to those noted earlier. The singular point of emphasis with student learning outcomes assessment is the assertion that there is a delta-change that the student learned something as a result of their interaction with you and your program. And hopefully, it is something you have identified as why your program is part of the larger student learning enterprise that resides at your community college. The larger student learning enterprise at most institutions is often articulated in the college's mission statement, vision statement, and institutional values, and these documents serve as a good foundation for identifying those outcomes in student learning you aspire to deliver to your students in your programs.

With this stated as an affirmation here, assessing programs related to student learning outcomes in our work can no longer be an optional activity for anyone in our profession. Our role as the principal advocates for the students and their learning depends on it. This change in how we approach our work will also allow the profession to stand alongside academic colleagues as equal partners in the student learning enterprise. And as new student life and services come online at community colleges, the need to demonstrate to senior leaders that student affairs professionals can produce results to show a return on the college's investment is essential to the future student affairs organization in the community college sector. It is clear that assessment activities that include student learning outcomes are a necessary component in the new community college student affairs organization.

The College With No Borders!

The final consideration is the need to expand the student affairs professional's current role as a community relations specialist into one that is more far-reaching into the multiple communities the community college serves. In Chapter 4, Hernandez and Hernández remind us of the important role the senior student affairs officer can play with community relations whether they are promoting traditional town-gown relationship or extensively involved in the complexity a region must deal with in advancing workforce development. Unlike other higher education sectors, student affairs professionals at community colleges must develop strong relationships with municipal, county, and state officials on topics such as workforce development and economic development. With the increased pressures to cross check closing the workforce skills gap with community college graduates, many student affairs professionals (beyond the career services professionals) will also have to build stronger connections with industry and corporate employers.

Community colleges have long been deemed institutions of higher education without borders or ivory towers to enclose their campus proper. Their success is directly tied to the employers they partner with in the workforce investment activities. Some of these activities are academic credential based while others are closer to the noncredit continuing education model. Senior campus leaders are largely involved in developing and maintaining these relationships, as are some faculty in discipline-specific activities (i.e., advance manufacturing and health-related fields). The community college student affairs role may be delimited to the career services areas. And albeit an important function, the federal and state push to close the medium- and high-tech skills gap in the American workforce expands the community colleges student affairs relationship beyond career development and into other elements, such as student internship, cooperatives, and other forms of applied learning opportunities with employers; and civic engagement projects that require students to problem solve community issues alongside employers and often municipal leaders. The community college professional also plays a critical role in maintaining "town-gown" relationships with municipal leaders and off-campus housing centers. The formation of college–community coalitions in the 1990s to curb underage drinking and disruptive conduct of students in residential neighborhoods has been replaced with community action groups where students and landlords, students and neighbors, and students and municipal leaders are hosting community events and programs to bring communities closer together and again where students invest time in taking ownership for solving problems in municipalities.

The development and maintenance of these municipal-based community coalitions and action groups takes a concerted and orchestrated effort. The leadership of this group invariably needs a community college student affairs professional on the team. They play a key role in educating the municipal constituents on the realities of community college life and often the legal, practical, and educational elements of student–community interactions and initiatives. And when these college–community groups are active and engaging, they do wonders for all involved. Community college professionals who are successful at this work have learned how to construct effective partnerships. The strength of these partnerships are determined where clearly delineated goals are developed and articulated to the community, wide community representation, articulated desired outcomes are revisited annually, communication strategies implemented and circulated widely, and finally, periodic assessment to determine if these community coalitions are accomplishing what they set out to accomplish. Representation in these coalitions include employers, business leaders, municipal leaders, student leaders, landlords, an array of college leaders and staff, law enforcement, community advocacy and service groups, and more students. They tend to emerge as prevention-minded, transition into intervention and problem-solving focused, and mature into community advocacy work. The central theme in their development is a movement from official driven to student/community operated and owned. When fully matured, they highlight the role of the community college does not end at the college entrance and that the student affairs professional is at the center of this outreach and community development effort.

References

Arminio, J., Carpenter, S., Dunn, M., Liddell, D., Janosik, S., Lowery, J., . . . Segawa, M. (2006). *Task force on certification: Preliminary report*. Washington, DC: ACPA.

Bresciani, M., Todd, D., Carpenter, S., Janosik, S., Komives, S., Love, P., . . . Tyrell, S. (2010). *ACPA/NASPA professional competency areas for student affairs practitioners*. Washington, DC: ACPA/NASPA.

NEW DIRECTIONS FOR COMMUNITY COLLEGES • DOI: 10.1002/cc

Hanson, G. R. (1988). Critical issues in the assessment of value added in education. In T. W. Banta (Ed.), *New Directions for Institutional Research: No. 59. Implementing outcomes assessment: Promise and perils* (pp. 53–67). San Francisco, CA: Jossey-Bass.

Janosik, S., & Carpenter, S. (2005). *A report to ACPA's task force on certification.* Washington, DC: American College Personnel Association.

Love, P., Carpenter, S., Haggerty, B., Hoffman, B., Janosik, S., Klein, S., … Wilson, M. (2007). *Professional competencies: A report of the Steering Committee on professional competencies.* Washington, DC: ACPA/NASPA.

Spellings Commission. (2006). *A test of leadership: Charting the course of U.S. higher education.* Washington, DC: U.S. Department of Education.

Tyrell, S., & Farmer, M. (2006, March). *A comparative analysis of mid-level managers' (and other staff in student affairs) skills and knowledge competencies.* Paper presented for the Mid Level Research Team, Commission on Administration Leadership, ACPA Convention, Indianapolis, IN.

Tyrell, S., Farmer, M., Fey, C., Zerwas, S., Perkins, R., Diana, R., & Zmich, R. (2005). *Survey on administrators' professional development needs.* Unpublished manuscript, Commission for Administrative Leadership, American College Personnel Association, Washington, DC.

Tyrell, S., & Fey, C. (Eds.). (in press). *Student affairs at a crossroads: Choosing a pathway toward transformation or maintaining the status quo.* Manuscript submitted for publication.

Walter, T., Fey, C., Cortese, P., & Borg, T. (1991, March). *Leaders of the student affairs profession: A perspective on mid-level managers.* Paper presented at the annual meeting of the American College Personnel Association, Atlanta, GA.

STEVE TYRELL *is the president of North Country Community College.*

9

In this final chapter, the authors synthesize and draw from chapters across this volume to provide concluding remarks and recommendations. The authors suggest that core to the discussion of excellence of student affairs in community colleges are the concepts of integration and collaboration. As professionals tasked with supporting the student learning experience at institutions with diverse, commuter populations, the formal and informal relationships and collaborations between student and academic affairs are critical.

Excellence Within Student Affairs: Understanding the Practice of Integrating Academic and Student Affairs

C. Casey Ozaki, Anne M. Hornak

The work of student affairs is critical across all institutional types, but essential at a community college, an open access institution. Open access contributes to student demographics that require more attention and support. Presently, students at community colleges make up approximately one-third of the undergraduate population in the United States (Knapp, Kelly-Reid, & Ginder, 2012). While the enrollments at community colleges are holding steady across the country, the students within this population require more assistance, both in and out of the classroom. The demographics of students entering community colleges shows that higher percentages of these students come from schools that are less likely to academically prepare students for higher education, have lower socioeconomic backgrounds, have parents with lower education levels, and require more developmental coursework. These characteristics have a strong relationship to persistence and success in higher education (Renn & Reason, 2012); however, these attributes are not insurmountable for success and, more importantly, have implications for the work and structure of student affairs. In order for student affairs practitioners and units to be responsive to the needs of a wide range of students, the work must involve an academic orientation and

NEW DIRECTIONS FOR COMMUNITY COLLEGES, no. 166, Summer 2014 © 2014 Wiley Periodicals, Inc.
Published online in Wiley Online Library (wileyonlinelibrary.com) • DOI: 10.1002/cc.20104

collaboration between student and academic affairs. In this chapter, we highlight the importance of the collaboration and integration of academic and student affairs goals and practice in these institutions in the pursuit of excellence and quality of education.

Excellence in Student Affairs

In the Editors' Notes and first chapter, the concept of "excellence" as a guiding framework and goal for educational quality is emphasized and discussed in relation to the two-year institution. Given the national spotlight and pressure to increase transfer and graduation rates, community college faculty and staff are being challenged to provide quality education that supports students through a two-year college to academic goal completion. While excellent educational quality is critical to all higher education, the completion agenda discourse has increasingly focused on the role of community colleges in the improvement of student success. For example, the White House Summit on Community Colleges in 2010 (http://www.ed.gov/college-completion/community-college-summit) hosted a focused discussion that highlighted community colleges as a critical entryway into postsecondary education for many students, students who may otherwise never attend college. Part of the summit included a white paper and forum intended to stimulate thought, conversation, and recommendations for the role of student services and student affairs in the completion agenda. These national conversations prime the atmosphere for scrutiny of educational quality. Excellence is a critical element for supporting student success. Yet, understanding what quality student affairs at a community college looks like is not as straightforward as one might hope. With an overarching goal of completion and educational success, how differing levels of professionals contribute will vary. In addition, many professional (i.e., student affairs) and institutional (i.e., accreditation) external organizations have implemented their own definitions and indicators of quality.

Throughout this volume, chapter authors explored quality student services practice in community college. What excellence is in higher education is going to vary widely dependent on institution, functional goals, and roles. For example, in Chapter 3 Tyrell discusses the control and management strategies that mid-managers might adopt and explores the impact that their choices and accompanying managerial identities have on their effectiveness. While in Chapter 4, Hernandez and Hernández describe critical roles of SSAO as that of manager, mediator, and educator, all of which focus on the person's ability to work with and supervise employees. They direct the reader to the AACC leadership competences and relevant student affairs organizations for developmental guidance on important abilities and skills, such as those described by the authors. Examining the influence of external guiding organizations on excellence, Hornak offers a roadmap to the standards as well as examples of the self-assessment guides in practice.

NEW DIRECTIONS FOR COMMUNITY COLLEGES • DOI: 10.1002/cc

The standards serve not in an accreditation role, but rather voluntary standards to guide practice and create a rigorous method for self-assessment and evaluation of programs. Similarly, in Chapter 6, Munsch and Cortez offer an overview of the ACPA/NASPA competencies that provide a guide to best practice for professionals. The chapter is limited in concrete examples of the competencies in action; however, we assert that because we do not name our work under these competencies, many professionals truly work from at least the basic to intermediate skill level. We invite leaders and supervisors to think about how to further incorporate the development of these skills into their ongoing professional development.

These examples demonstrate how expectations, abilities, and competencies for student affairs professionals and practice in community colleges often overlap depending on one's particular lens, but they are also varied and nuanced depending on those same lenses.

Excellence as Academic and Student Affairs Integration and Collaboration

While traditional student affairs functions exist at community colleges, there is a much greater emphasis on the academic activity and purpose of these institutional types in order to meet the needs of their varied student population. Therefore, student affairs departments and services are intertwined with the academic affairs units and work of the institution. At two-year colleges, the goals and purposes of student affairs are intertwined with academic work, even more so than one might traditionally see on a four-year campus. Collaborations, cross-training, information sharing, and partnerships across student and academic affairs are endemic to the work of the institution. To this end, it is not uncommon for student affairs units to be organizationally housed under academic affairs reporting lines.

Within community colleges, it is necessary for all entities to work together to support the students and their academic goals. Therefore, to be "excellent" in student affairs at two-year institutions practice must include collaboration and innovation. In 2009, the Pathways to College Network published a report for the Institute for Higher Education Policy about *Removing Roadblocks to Rigor: Linking Academic and Social Supports to Ensure College Readiness and Success*. In this report, authors argue that critical to a student's success is the availability of a network of academic and social support, particularly while implementing high standards and rigor. They state, "A detailed understanding of the types of academic and social support and how they work in tandem with academic standards must be a part of these conversations" (Pathways to College Network, 2009, p. 1). The importance of this observation is underscored by the recommendation to "integrate and coordinate academic and social support strategies focused on enabling students to meet rigorous academic standards" (p. 3). This report identified academic and social support services as equally important for student success and critical to the goals of excellence in education and success.

This call for aligning student and academic affairs work through collaborations, partnerships, and formal and informal cross-institutional relationships has also been echoed in the literature and national conversations on the topic. The White House Summit on Community Colleges' white paper (Cooper, 2010), *Student Support Services at Community Colleges: A Strategy for Increasing Student Persistence and Attainment,* concluded that,

> In a study of effective strategies for student service programs at community colleges, it was recommended that institutions offer more 'enhanced student services.' Such programs would then be linked to other services, but also integrated into existing campus wide reform strategies, thereby allowing student services to be offered, in a coordinated fashion and over an extended period of time. Since many students encounter ongoing challenges throughout their academic career—related to academic, social, and financial needs—it is imperative to offer students linked and sustained services in all areas of the college. (p. 25)

Integration of academic and student services across campus is recognized as a critical approach to providing quality education and support to promote student completion. Movement to more partnerships and collaborations on campuses also has implications for the staff and leaders. Amey's (2010) article on collaboration competencies for community college leaders recognizes the increasing frequency of collaborations used as a strategy to meet the needs of multiple constituencies on campus. Finally, the American Association for Community Colleges also suggests that 21st century community college leaders need to develop their skills and abilities in six competency areas, one of which is to be able to collaborate. While integration, collaboration, and partnerships have likely been a historical part of the work in student services at community colleges, in recent years integration and collaboration has been a recommended strategy of choice for quality education.

Throughout this volume, there were examples of how student affairs departments and functional areas demonstrate excellence—across different position types and through an exploration of the standards and expectations that external organizations promote for excellence in higher education and student affairs broadly. The character of student affairs as an integrated academic-focused enterprise that utilizes cross-function relationships and work is underscored. For example, in Tyrell's discussion of mid-managers in Chapter 3, he promotes the importance of, and often most effective, a collaborative managerial approach that not only allows for constructive exploration of differences but flexibility in who is part of that collaborative team—often including individuals beyond the student affairs and services designation. In Chapter 2, Lunceford describes how during a recent reorganization a student affairs unit was placed under an academic affairs reporting line. This allows services like advising, which are considered student affairs programs but are intimately involved with academics, to have greater access to academic leadership and integrate both student and academic affairs in their practice.

The essential elements of effective collaborations include leadership and oversight from both academic affairs and student affairs. These individuals need to understand both the curricular goals of the program as well as the cocurricular outcomes. Additionally, they must ensure that programs are meeting their intended learning outcomes and that those connect to the broader vision and goals of the institution. Other essential elements of effective collaborations include the use of strong student leaders, supportive faculty, and college administrators that are program champions. The use of strong student leaders can increase program visibility and offer students a voice in planning. Supportive faculty are always critical and at community colleges this can be challenging since many faculty are adjunct or part time. Collaborations that are successful include committed faculty who provide a link between the divisions, but also a voice in the academic mission of the college. These linkages are critical across both academic and student affairs, but it is crucial that colleges capitalize on the connections between in- and out-of-class learning experiences.

Conclusion

As the work of student affairs professionals rapidly changes at community colleges, it is essential that colleges define their own metrics to define excellence. In this volume, the authors explored many aspects of excellence in student affairs at community colleges. The definition of excellence cuts across standards, competencies, professional levels, and roles at the college. The contributions of student affairs professionals can be difficult to define and measure at many colleges. Most professionals work across functions and units, and the work tends to be characterized as ancillary to the core mission of educating students. The authors in this volume reinforce the importance of the use of standards and competencies in data collection and evaluation of student affairs functions. Yet, the content in this volume also recognizes that professional excellence will vary by career stages and is, and should be, embedded and defined by the local campus-level. Many of the chapters in this volume include examples of exemplary work in student affairs, it is important to note that we also understand much still needs to be done. We offer this volume as both a practical example of what is occurring at community colleges, but also as an aspirational example of where community college student affairs needs to be to call themselves gold standard programs.

References

Amey, M. J. (2010). Leading partnerships: Competencies for collaboration. In D. L. Wallin (Ed.), *New Directions for Community Colleges: No. 149. Leadership in an era of change* (pp. 13–23). San Francisco, CA: Jossey-Bass. doi:10.1002/cc.391

Cooper, M. (2010, October). *Student support services at community colleges: A strategy for increasing student persistence and attainment.* Paper presented at the White House Summit on Community Colleges. Retrieved from http://www2 .ed.gov/PDFDocs/college-completion/04-student-support-services-at-community -colleges.pdf

Knapp, L. G., Kelly-Reid, J. E., & Ginder, S. A. (2012). *Enrollment in postsecondary institutions, Fall 2011; Financial statistics, fiscal year 2011; and graduate rates, selected cohorts, 2003–2008: First look (provisional data)* (NCES 2012-174rev). Washington, DC: U.S. Department of Education, National Central for Education Statistics. Retrieved from http://nces.ed.gov/pubs2012/2012174rev.pdf

Pathways to College Network. (2009). *Removing roadblocks to rigor: Linking academic and social supports to ensure college readiness and success.* Washington, DC: Institute for Higher Education Policy. Retrieved from http://www.ihep.org/assets/files/programs /pcn/Roadblocks.pdf

Renn, K. A., & Reason, R. D. (2012). *College students in the United States: Characteristics, experiences, and outcomes.* San Francisco, CA: Jossey-Bass.

C. CASEY OZAKI *is an assistant professor of teaching and learning at the University of North Dakota.*

ANNE M. HORNAK *is an associate professor of educational leadership at Central Michigan University.*

INDEX

OTHER TITLES AVAILABLE IN THE
New Directions for Community Colleges
ARTHUR M. COHEN, EDITOR-IN-CHIEF
CAROLINE Q. DURDELLA AND NATHAN R. DURDELLA, ASSOCIATE EDITORS

CC165 **Strengthening Community Colleges Through Institutional Collaborations**
Michael J. Roggow
Institutional collaborations are cornerstones for building successful programs that support effective teaching and learning, quality advisement, global awareness, community building, and institutional advancement. Partnerships call for individual and collective thinking and planning—essential building blocks for designing best practices and integrating college communities. This issue of *New Directions for Community Colleges* illustrates various examples of effective collaborations written by community college presidents, administrators, faculty, and leaders of state governments and national organizations. Each has contributed a story illustrating a successful program that required the efforts of a range of individuals, and recommendations for others to build their own successes. Their topics include:

- How to build effective dual enrollment programs to motivate high school students in rural areas to pursue higher education
- Why collaboration is crucial for institutions that apply for federal grant funding
- Effective partnering with institutional research and technology departments to advance student services and college-wide strategic planning
- How to infuse service learning into curricula to engage and encourage minority students at community colleges to focus their career aspirations based on their internship experiences
- How to advance community college study abroad programs through collective participation of administrators and faculty, and outside organizations
- Creating and sustaining effective partnerships between a state and its local colleges

The chapters in this volume were written to inform administrators and faculty about myriad ways to accomplish college-wide goals by reaching across institutional divisions and to outside organizations to form effective, productive partnerships.
ISBN: 978-11188-81453

CC164 **The College Completion Agenda: Practical Approaches for Reaching the Big Goal**
Brad C. Phillips, Jordan E. Horowitz
This volume of *New Directions for Community Colleges* provides practical ways colleges can focus on the College Completion Agenda. Originally begun as an economic workforce issue for the Obama administration, the College Completion Agenda has been adopted by myriad educational institutions, public and private funders, and others. The identified "Big Goal" is to

increase the proportion of Americans with high quality college degrees and credentials from 39% of the population to 60% by 2025. To date, much advice has been offered to colleges about what the issues are and what needs to be done. However, there is considerable work being done at colleges around the country to address the identified issues. This volume introduces some of these policies and practices—the thinking behind them, research supporting them, roles to be fulfilled, and impact on the student experience. ISBN: 978-11188-62162

CC163 **Fostering the Liberal Arts in the 21st-Century Community College**
Keith Kroll
The founding mission of the public, comprehensive community college included vocational training, developmental education, community education, and its collegiate function: transfer and the liberal arts. Early on in its history, however, the community colleges mission began to drift toward vocational training to such an extent that at the local, state, and national level the dominant narrative of the 21st-century community college portrays a job (re)training center more than an educational institution. While numerous books have described the growing threat to the liberal arts in 4-year colleges and universities, the response to "mission shift" within the community college has been muted. This volume offers a timely, much-needed, and persuasive argument for the importance of a liberal arts education, particularly in the humanities, for all students attending a public, comprehensive community college. ISBN: 978-11188-34558

CC162 **The Future of the Urban Community College: Shaping the Pathways to a Multiracial Democracy**
Gunder Myran, Curtis L. Ivery, Michael H. Parsons, Charles Kinsley
America's biggest cities are pulse points for the entire country. Already weakened by decades of decline, their uneven recovery from the recent Great Recession has resulted in the further concentration of prosperity in a few and hardship for all the rest. Their citizens similarly reflect widening disparity between the wealthiest and poorest, threatening an endangered middle class that used to be the proudest measure of our economic and democratic ideals.

Urban community colleges are undergoing rapid, multidimensional changes in response to the new conditions and demands everywhere. The challenge for all, regardless of size or location, is to reinvent themselves so they can better meet the particular needs of their respective communities. This national higher-education mandate is vital to democracy itself, especially given the multiracial nature of metropolitan areas, where challenges and opportunities have always been most pronounced.

The future is as unpredictable as the events that brought us to this critical juncture. Spurred by outside pressure and support as well as deep commitment from within, urban colleges are vigorously exploring new strategies for sustainability and success. In this volume, some of the most prominent practitioners examine every major aspect of the change-engagement process, including the role of governing boards, workforce development, community partnerships, and redesign of outdated business and finance models. ISBN: 978-11188-06982

NEW DIRECTIONS FOR COMMUNITY COLLEGE
ORDER FORM SUBSCRIPTION AND SINGLE ISSUES

DISCOUNTED BACK ISSUES:

Use this form to receive 20% off all back issues of *New Directions for Community College*.
All single issues priced at **$23.20** (normally $29.00)

TITLE	ISSUE NO.	ISBN

Call 888-378-2537 or see mailing instructions below. When calling, mention the promotional code JBNND to receive your discount. For a complete list of issues, please visit www.josseybass.com/go/ndcc

SUBSCRIPTIONS: (1 YEAR, 4 ISSUES)

☐ New Order   ☐ Renewal

U.S.	☐ Individual: $89	☐ Institutional: $311
Canada/Mexico	☐ Individual: $89	☐ Institutional: $351
All Others	☐ Individual: $113	☐ Institutional: $385

Call 888-378-2537 or see mailing and pricing instructions below.
Online subscriptions are available at www.onlinelibrary.wiley.com

ORDER TOTALS:

Issue / Subscription Amount: $ _____

Shipping Amount: $ _____
(for single issues only – subscription prices include shipping)

Total Amount: $ _____

SHIPPING CHARGES:

First Item $6.00
Each Add'l Item $2.00

(No sales tax for U.S. subscriptions. Canadian residents, add GST for subscription orders. Individual rate subscriptions must be paid by personal check or credit card. Individual rate subscriptions may not be resold as library copies.)

BILLING & SHIPPING INFORMATION:

☐ **PAYMENT ENCLOSED:** *(U.S. check or money order only. All payments must be in U.S. dollars.)*

☐ **CREDIT CARD:** ☐ VISA ☐ MC ☐ AMEX

Card number _____Exp. Date_____

Card Holder Name_____Card Issue #_____

Signature _____Day Phone_____

☐ **BILL ME:** *(U.S. institutional orders only. Purchase order required.)*

Purchase order # _____
    Federal Tax ID 13559302 • GST 89102-8052

Name_____

Address_____

Phone_____ E-mail_____

Copy or detach page and send to: **John Wiley & Sons, One Montgomery Street, Suite 1200, San Francisco, CA 94104-4594**

Order Form can also be faxed to: **888-481-2665**

PROMO JBNND

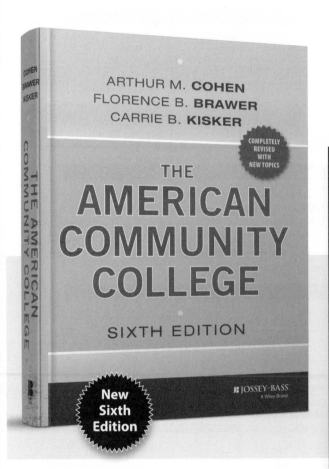

ARTHUR M. **COHEN**
FLORENCE B. **BRAWER**
CARRIE B. **KISKER**

COMPLETELY REVISED WITH NEW TOPICS

THE
AMERICAN COMMUNITY COLLEGE

SIXTH EDITION

JOSSEY-BASS
A Wiley Brand

New Sixth Edition

For over thirty years, *The American Community College* has provided up-to-date information and statistics about community colleges. It has been widely used in graduate courses and by community college scholars, institutional researchers, and on-the-ground administrators.

The sixth edition has been significantly updated with discussions of current issues including:

• Outcomes and accountability

• The rise of for-profit colleges

• Leadership and administrative challenges

• Revenue generation

• Distance learning

The book concludes with a cogent response to contempora criticisms of the institution.

JOSSEY-BASS
A Wiley Bran